ATOMIC

STEPS

WIN BIG OR GO HOME

JOHN ALAN ANDREWS

Copyright © 2023 by John A. Andrews
ISBN: 9798866470839
Cover Art: ALI
Cover Photo: Adrian Carr
All rights reserved.

ATOMIC STEPS

TABLE OF CONTENTS

PREFACE...3
INTRODUCTION..6
THE COMMITTMENT FACTOR...11
CHANGING YOUR THOUGHTS...27
CHANGING YOUR WORDS..46
CHANGING YOUR ACTIONS..56
BREAKING FREE..76
PREPAREDNESS...86
BELIEF...93
MOMENTUM...99
VISION..103
TIMING..115
PURPOSE...122
PASSION...132
PERSONALITY...142
MINDSET...148
TEAMSPORT...161
BURNING YOUR SHIPS..165
COMMITTED TO FLY..191
THE END IN MIND...197
CHANGING YOUR CHARACTER...206
CHANGING THE WORLD..225
LEGACY DEFINED..234

AUDIOBOOK – NOW STREAMING
@

ALIPNET
ORIGINAL

ATOMIC STEPS

PREFACE

During the Cannes Film Festival of 2023, I visited Nice and Monaco, nearby regions of Southern France. On this trip, I caught the vision for drafting a twisted Crime thriller, cemented in the enclaves of those three cities.

Before the Cannes Festival wrapped, I found myself sitting in a room where studio execs were poised to discuss Filming in those localities and on the studio lot. I asked myself: *Was this really happening?*

It was my fourth meeting of the day, and after the third meeting, I said to myself:

I've had enough lecturing for one day. It is time to return to my booth and entertain prospective clients. After all, that's why I attended the event, I reckoned.

Even so, I felt belonged and sat in for meeting number four. You see, I have the voraciousness for the movie studio. You say movie studios and I am tickled – Quora.

The studio execs did their spiel. In my mind, the dots were connecting. I saw endless possibilities. My hand immediately went up when the speaker took a breather for questions. I proceeded by asking tough questions regarding the sustainability or longevity of that market and its packaging. If they were ready to launch out, so was I.

ATOMIC STEPS

I returned to New York, and amid fighting off the naysayers of my vision, I went to work –drafting the police procedural thriller. As a result, in less than four months, I returned to France at the Studios' invitation and sat in for a meeting, a tour, plus a luncheon to discuss the upcoming TV series. It is said,

"Luck is where preparedness meets with opportunity."

When a champion wants something, they go after it with all they can muster. "Bring it on," he says. "Lead me through the unknown. There I will discover myself and others. If it has never been done, I will create it. If it demands training, I will become coachable. The tougher it becomes the better I like it. If it must be it is up to me. Therefore, I will "Man up." If I go down, it will not happen because I wimped out - If I go down, I'm going down fighting. I possess a "pit bull" mentality because I was born to win!" Champions look for something to latch on to, a dream, a vision, a cause.

"Give it to me and watch what I will do with it," they demand. If the team desires a touchdown, they crave the interception and cradle that ball into the end zone.

Ironically, that play may not have been drawn up or happenstance. However, it has been drafted and executed over and over again, analogous to the baby

ATOMIC STEPS

steps syndrome. Those steps eventually mature into "the catch me if you can" scenario.

Doing the mundane is not always comfortable. We often complain about how boring it is to do the same thing repeatedly. Yet, champions do the same things repeatedly to win a championship. They become adept at mastering the mundane.

GET READY TO CHALLENGE your excuses after the first read of this step-climbing order. With every read, plus application, you are destined to build expansive character... Your mantra should echo:

I can. I will and shall not be denied...

I am not sure you'll be able to walk on water or perform earthshaking miracles, but in your imagination, you just might create wonders. The doors should swing open to you, giving you a seat at the table. What you touch should turn to gold during your ascent. This compilation, if used as your study guide, could be the most comprehensive book on the laws of power and success to ever grace your personal library. Do not allow it to accumulate dust on the shelf.

- John Alan. Andrews

ATOMIC STEPS

INTRODUCTION

It has become very apparent that we live in the microwave age. One of the instant meals, the instant this and instant that. We get on a plane in Los Angeles or New York and within hours we arrive in Europe. We rush to work, rush back home, and gulp down our food. Make the gesture for the sign of the cross. We settle for a snack of type sexual interlude instead of a buffet. We got married today and divorced right after the honeymoon. Everything happens so fast, and we do not seem to embrace the commitment mindset.

In all this mad rush, we toss our values into an abyss. Our dreams and goals plummet with that miscalculated nosedive. Our *commitment* to our vision and to others becomes short-lived. We blame the system, the economy, our lover, our parents, our kids, the devil, and even God gets thrown into the mix sometimes. We inadvertently kick the cat. We lose the good we might win by failing to commit to anything, therefore we settle for anything. As a result, we spend our lives sitting on the fence.

A champion, on the other hand, spends time working on himself. He knows that if he fails to prepare, he has by choice prepared to fail. He must be his best. Therefore, he commits, knowing that

ATOMIC STEPS

winning is an all-time thing, according to Vince Lombardi.

Whenever I think of commitment, my mind goes back to the airplane taxiing down the runway scenario. Prior to taking off, the pilot receives permission from the air traffic control tower. He then engages the aircraft, it picks up speed, engages the sky and the landing gear retracts as it becomes airborne. As it gains altitude, passengers are instructed to unfasten their seatbelts - refreshments are served. The pilot announces the estimated time of arrival and the weather in that city of destination. That plane is now committed to flying. There is an end, in mind.

Another story I once heard helps put commitment into perspective. One day a chicken and a pig were riding in a taxi. Simultaneously, they noticed a billboard displaying "The Great American Breakfast" (bacon and eggs). The chicken looks across at the pig and remarks,

" Look at us up there! That is impressive, isn't it?" The pig with no time to waste responds,

"For you, it's all in a day's work but for me, it's total commitment."

The chicken was involved but the pig was committed. We find that at times commitment could require all you've got.

ATOMIC STEPS

In 1963, the late Dr. Martin Luther King Jr. while addressing a segment of the American populous echoed, "If a man hasn't discovered something that he will die for, he isn't fit to live."

King's life was saturated with a cause greater than self. His cause required all or nothing. That is a champion's mindset.

"There's only one way to succeed in anything, and that is to give it everything. I do, and I demand that my players do, "

echoed Vince Lombardi, the late coach of the Green Bay Packers.

No wonder he was one of the best to ever coach the game of football.

On Feb. 2, 1959, Lombardi arrived in Green Bay and told the committee, "I want it understood that I am in complete command here." His commitment to the game helped to totally transform the Green Bay Packers back then.

In the early part of 1959, the Packers were coming off a 1-10-1 season -- the worst in team history. Winners of six NFL championships during the Curly Lambeau era, the Packers hadn't had a winning season since 1947. Lombardi's first season with the Packers was a stunning success, turning that 1-10-1 team of 1958 into a 7-5 team in 1959 and picking up unanimous Coach of the Year honors in the process. His first game with the Packers was a 9-6 victory

ATOMIC STEPS

over the Chicago Bears in the new City Stadium -- later to be renamed Lambeau Field -- and when it was over, the players carried their head coach off the field in triumph.

ATOMIC STEPS

"Until one is committed, there is hesitance, the chance to draw back. Always ineffectiveness. Concerning all acts of initiative (and creation), there is one elemental truth, the ignorance of which kills countless ideas and splendid plans; that the moment one commits oneself, then providence moves too. All sorts of things occur to help one that would never have otherwise occurred. A whole stream of events issues from the decision, raising in one's favor all manner of unforeseen incidents and meetings and material assistance which no man could have dreamed would come his way. Whatever you can do or dream you can begin it. Genius has boldness power and magic in it. Begin now."

- Goethe

1

THE COMMITMENT FACTOR

Martin Luther King Jr., one of the greatest dreamers who ever lived, declared: "Take the first step in faith. You don't have to see the whole staircase. Just take the first step."

I have encountered scores of individuals stepping into my life for a reason, some for a season, and others for a lifetime. The masses have talked the talk, others have walked the walk, but the chosen have done both.

Each brought with them a reflection of the experiences — good, bad, and ugly that they've encountered traversing along life's corridor. They weren't born the person they grew to become.

ATOMIC STEPS

Rather, day-by-day and year-by-year, they acquired their definition from the books they read, the thoughts they entertained, and the people with whom they've associated.

There's truth to this maxim:

"Show me your friends and I'll tell you who you are."

If you spend time together with bank robbers you could end up driving the getaway car, and if you associate with pigs, you'll soon be rolling in the mud. Kids who wind up in gangs join them primarily to fulfill a need for community, and soon, they prey on society to support that community and attain identity within the group. Through conversion to Christianity, though, a Gangbanger can dust himself off to lead a church or become a mentor to struggling youth.

Paul, once a persecutor of Christians, encountered a changed life on the road to Damascus when struck by a bright light from heaven.

Following three days of blindness, he regained his sight by the hand of a disciple named Ananias, and immediately turned his life around, preaching Jesus as the Son of God (Acts 9:1-20).

So, yes, you can become the person you desire to become. Is it going to be easy? Probably not, effective change is not a Jack and the Beanstalk scenario. It's more like a seasonal transition.

ATOMIC STEPS

During autumn, leaves die and fall to the ground before winter steps in, and like the seasons, change is a process. Real change doesn't happen overnight.

It is said that a person can make or break a habit in 21 days. Although some characters demand a more expansive arch.

Becoming who you want to become is going to take work, as does raising a child, building a successful marriage, getting a degree, or mastering a craft. Is it possible? It has been done. Can you, do it? Only if you think you can. Will you lift yourself by your bootstraps? Leaders aren't born; they are made. Is the change worth the effort? Real change starts on the inside. According to James Allen,

"You cannot travel within and stand still without."

Your greatest achievement was at first, and for a while, just a thought. Every invention originated from someone's thoughts, even this book that you are holding in your hands. Thomas Edison made more than 1,000 unsuccessful attempts to develop the lightbulb which you are probably using to read these pages. The first highlighter, a replica of the one that you are probably using to highlight those key points from these pages, was invented by Dr. Frank Honn in 1962.

ATOMIC STEPS

Which cause(s) are you willing to commit to during your lifetime? Total commitment, which is the mindset of Champions, warrants a cause greater than self. One must see that the cause is greater than themselves. They step into the game of life versus watching from the sidelines.

Later in this volume, I'll give you the basic formula for a champion's mindset.

Imagine if you were stricken with cancer, and as your physician, I were to tell you that the cure for your almost fatal disease lies beneath the riverbed. What if I prescribed that if you found a little smooth rock, glittering as a diamond, placed it twice a day outside the cancer-infected area for one month, and you would be cured? What time would you wake up in the morning and what time would you arrive at the riverbed?

As you look in the water, noticing multiple stones ruggedly, and smoothly shaped, would you use a net or your bare hands, so you can feel the contour and identify your cure easily?

To ensure your success and beat the odds, let's say you decided to use your hands. Sunset came and you didn't find it, now with blistered fingers, and an angry facial disposition, you are still without. Would you focus on returning the following day to continue your search?

ATOMIC STEPS

If you did? By now you have cleared almost all the stones from that riverbed, but that special stone was yet to be found. Not only are your hands still aching and bloodied, but your back hurts severely. The sun sets again. You drag yourself home, wanting to admit defeat. Tension mounts, as the place where your disease nestles aggravates you. Recoiling you weigh your options: Kemo or finding that stone? You catapult into a state of withdrawal.

Now furious about the price you have paid thus far, you pick up the phone and call me complaining,

"Where is that stone? I've looked all over; I'm sore. It's nowhere to be found." And I respond, "Keep looking, the stone is there, plus you need to start medicating tomorrow."

Now you jump out of bed before dawn, so you can get to that riverbed, fearing that a high tide of water will wash your medication away.

Then right before sunset, amid cold sweat, with what little energy you have left, you feebly clear more rocks from that riverbed. Just when you were about to give up, you discovered the smooth stone - the cure for your disease. With one hand covering your mouth in exhilaration and the other riveted to the stone, in a Hallelujah moment. Knowing that you have a whole month of treatment to go, you

ATOMIC STEPS

feel as though you've already been cured. You call me back jubilantly.

Forgetting the pain you've gone through, you shout out,

"I've found it, I've found it! I love you, doctor. Thanks for saving my life."

I respond.

"YOU did it! What a thrill of success. Now you can be cured of your disease. You committed to the process and now you have success. YES!"

Author Berton Braley had this to say:

"If you want a thing bad enough to go out and fight for it, to work day and night for it, to give up your time, and your sleep for it…if all that you dream and the scheme is about it, and life seems useless and worthless without it…if you gladly sweat for it and fret for it and plan for it and lose all your terror of opposition for it…if you simply go after that thing you want with all of your capacity, strength and sagacity, faith, hope and confidence, and stern pertinacity…if neither cold, poverty, famine, nor gout, sickness nor pain, of body and brain, can keep you away from the thing that you want…if dogged and grim you beseech it, with the help of God, you WILL get it!"

On Friday, January 20th, 1961, President John F. Kennedy, America's youngest president, announced after a heavy snowfall the night before

ATOMIC STEPS

his inauguration.

"I do not shrink from this responsibility – I welcome it"

On May 25th, 1961, months later, he announced in an address to Congress that America would be the first country to put a man on the moon.

He explained,

"I believe we possess all the resources and talents necessary. But the facts of the matter are that we have never made the national decisions or marshaled the national resources required for such leadership. We have never specified long-range goals on an urgent time schedule or managed our resources and our time to ensure their fulfillment."

Plans for this mission gradually began to unfold, and suddenly everything at NASA jumped into momentum mode. Productivity stepped up drastically, and finally, on July 20, 1969, Neil Armstrong became the first man to set foot on the moon. The vision was realized. America as a nation had once again beaten the odds.

Oftentimes, I have seen individuals loaded with potential who fail to grasp a leader's vision. Fear of commitment is one of the main causes of the lazy man's disease known as "fence-sitting." Lack of commitment in any relationship could be attributed to the inability to tie into the vision of the other person. That lack results in an unfulfilled dream.

ATOMIC STEPS

When people jump on board a leader's vision, like they did back at NASA, then momentum emerges, and the organization becomes unstoppable. There always seems to be something extra that radiates from someone once they commit. It is the glue that bonds that entity together, creating constructive collaboration within the group. This makes it easier to turn the vision into reality.

In life, we find that when we are interested in something we tend to do it when it is convenient. When we are committed, we do it no matter what stands in our way – regardless of the crisis. How would you respond? If you were told that there was an automobile accident and one person got run over. How would you respond? On the other hand, if you were informed that it was your neighbor, how would you respond? If you were told that it was your neighbor's child who got run over, how would you respond? However, if you were told that it was your child what would your response be? I heard the story about a 95-pound woman who attempted to lift a bus off her little boy, she was committed to saving her son.

Have you ever met people who delight in sitting on their "good intentions?" They boast,

"I have a cause; I have been thinking about it since I was five years old. Someday I'll make it happen. When it gets launched, it will totally save the world.

ATOMIC STEPS

It is the best thing since sliced bread." Unfortunately, they never do anything about it. Their ship never sets sail. It is still tied to the dock. Those individuals are known as the "tomorrow people." They wait for the world to come to them Instead of meeting it head-on. They tell you, plainly, that they will start tomorrow. The problem arises, that tomorrow turns into another tomorrow, and then another tomorrow and another. "Sitting on the fence philosophy" and mindset does not guarantee them a launch. They never seem to grasp the fact that it is what you do about your vision that counts. Total commitment allows you to move toward your world, enabling it to move toward you. When you *launch* out, you create waves, and only by doing so can you attract committed energy into your sail.

I was moved over a year ago to author a book on relationships. I have realized that there are so many struggles in this area. Why? They allow their love to sit on the fence, rather than putting it into action. They dangle around the perimeter of that affair as if waiting for someone better to appear. For them, getting to know each other is just a façade. With no commitment between those two people whether in thought, word, or action love is forced to sit on the fence. The match and the coal usually must agree for the coal to burn. It's a known fact that if you want the fireplace to give you heat, you must keep feeding it wood.

In our society today, it's startling to find so many who spend the bulk of their life fence-sitting. They babysit this habit. They are afraid of what others will think or say if they were to decide to live outside of their comfort zone. They are afraid to leave their nest because stepping out requires decision-making. Decisions are non-negotiable to fulfill one another's needs - the basis of love.

Even if these needs keep on changing, as we grow, we change. So do our needs and the needs of the one loved. A relationship thrives on spreading love in layers, thus building a relationship that becomes unshakable. Don't we all wish that relationships were taught in schools? Instead, like parenting and finances we must learn it for ourselves.

The masses are looking for love on all the wrong faces and in all the wrong places. Including adults with failed relationship after relationship, leading to a world filled with envy and hatred.

What really is Love? What is this all-powerful emotion which makes one give up his crown for the one he loves? In his book *Think and Grow Rich* Napoleon Hill introduces us to Mrs. Wallis Simpson who caused the king to relinquish his crown for her love. Wallis possessed a burning desire to find a mate and carefully searched every step of the way. Her

ATOMIC STEPS

primary pursuit was love. She knew exactly what she wanted, not after she met the Prince of Wales, but long before. Despite her failure to find it twice, she had courage enough to continue. Though shadowed by her obscurity, Wallis triumphed over long odds until she finally met the king.

Love will cause one to go to other limits as in the case of the characters Romeo and Juliet, according to Shakespeare. **Love** is by far the most powerful force on earth. "For love, we will climb mountains, cross seas, traverse desert sands, and endure hardships. Without love, mountains become unclimbable, seas uncrossable, deserts unbearable, and hardships our plight in life."

States Dr. Gary Chapman in his book *The Five Love Languages*.

Every relationship needs commitment in it, for it to grow. When the focus is love, we raise our standards, experiencing a higher and deeper love. Without love in a relationship, there is no momentum, and without momentum, there is no belief. Without belief, there is no progress, and without progress, there is no success.

The masses quit at the first sign of defeat. They fail to hang in there a little longer to see results. Therefore, they miss the necessary experience to become all they can be.

ATOMIC STEPS

WILMA RUDOLPH was stricken with polio disease at four years old. This disease usually causes people to be crippled and unable to walk. Born in poverty, her parents could not afford good medical care. To make matters worse, she was from a large family – the 20th child of 22 children. Her dad was a railroad porter, and her mom was a housekeeper.

Her mom decided she would do whatever it took to help Wilma walk again. Despite the doctors saying that she would not be able to walk, her mom persisted, trying to beat the odds. She took her every week on a long bus trip to a hospital to receive therapy.

Wilma's condition didn't change, but the doctors told her mom that she needed to give Wilma a massage every day by rubbing her legs. She even taught Wilma's siblings how to do it, and they also rubbed her legs four times a day.

By the time Wilma turned 8, she could walk with a leg brace. After that, she was able to use a high-top shoe to support her foot. Wilma played basketball with her brothers every day.

One day, three years later Wilma's mom came home and found her playing basketball, not only by herself but *barefooted* without the aid of the special shoe.

A track coach encouraged Wilma to start running. She did and ran so well in her senior year in high

ATOMIC STEPS

school, that she qualified for the 1956 Olympics in Melbourne, Australia. There she won a bronze medal in the women's 400-meter relay.

In 1959, she qualified for the 1960 Olympic Games in Rome, by setting a world record in the 200-meter race. At the Olympics that year, she won two gold medals: one for the 100-meter race and one for the 200-meter race.

Then accidentally, she sprained her ankle, but Wilma ignored the pain and helped her team to win *another* gold medal for the 400-meter relay! She won 3 gold medals in the Rome Olympics.

She retired from running at age 22 but went on to coach women's track teams and encourage young people.

Wilma believed that God had a greater purpose for her, so she started the Wilma Rudolph Foundation.

She passed on because of brain cancer in 1994, but her influence still lives on in the lives of so many young people, who look up to her leadership.

One thing is for sure: If you grasp and apply these steps that I'm about to give you, not only will you climb to insurmountable heights in your life and career, but you'll also have more joy, more friends, more love, more money, more passion, and a deep sense of spiritual and intellectual satisfaction.

As your guide, I must prepare you with simple guidelines. Upon receiving the idea to draft my first

ATOMIC STEPS

book: The 5 Steps to Changing Your Life, inspirational thoughts flooded my mind, allowing me to complete its first draft in one week. To get the most out of this extended version, you need passion, blended with a burning desire to step up and take your ball into the end zone. Dare anyone to stop you.

DON'T QUIT

When things go wrong, as they sometimes will,
When the road you're trudging seems all uphill,
When the funds are low and the debts are high,
And you want to smile, but you have to sigh,
When care is pressing you down a bit,
Rest, if you must-but don't you quit.

Life is queer with its twists and turns,
As everyone of us sometimes learns,
And many a failure turns about.
When he might have won had he stuck it out.
Don't give up though the pace seems slow-

ATOMIC STEPS

You might succeed with another
blow.

Often the goal is nearer than
It seems to a faint and faltering
man,
Often the struggler has given
up.
When he might have captured
the victor's cup.
And learned too late, when the
night slipped down,
How close he was to the victor's
crown.

Success is failure turned inside
out-
The silver tint of the clouds of
doubt-
And you never can tell how
close you are,
It might be near when it seems
afar.
So, stick to the fight when
you're hardest hit-
It's when things seem worst that
you mustn't quit.

- Unknown

If you're ready to take on the world, you should commit to reading this book in its entirety. Do not

ATOMIC STEPS

half-step or create a dam; as a stream of water desires to reach the ocean, train yourself to do likewise. Once you've finished reading, re-read these steps as a refresher course. I'll see you at the summit of life's staircase.

2

CHANGING YOUR THOUGHTS

The sources of our drinking water are always heavily guarded and protected from intrusion and contaminants. People protect their bodies from the weather and other elements. And yet, few take the time to protect their thought source — the mind.

Imagine your best friend comes over to visit one day, and in his hands are two heavy bags. You offer him a seat, and then sit on your recliner and adjust it to a comfortable position.

"What's in the bags?"

ATOMIC STEPS

the one thing over which you have absolute control; only you can decide what you do with your thoughts.

Your way of thinking starts with individual thoughts, whether good, bad, or ugly. Your subconscious produces thought, and your five senses give birth to thought based on your present environment. God and the devil are the two other sources of thought.

The five senses deal with the mind, but God deals with the heart and speaks to us through the Holy Spirit. After Jesus' ascension into heaven, his disciples received the outpouring of the Holy Spirit from God and thus performed miraculous deeds. "God says: 'In the last days I will pour out of my Spirit on all kinds of people. Your sons and daughters will prophesy. Your young men will see visions, and your old men will dream dreams.'" (Acts 2:17) In most cases, the mind must be ready to utilize thoughts from God, just like the ground must be prepared before seeds are sown therein.

Thoughts enter your mind whether you want them to or not. They arrive at every waking and sleeping moment of your life, as both initial data and original ideas and sometimes turn into action. In his book *Hung by the Tongue*, author Francis P. Martin explains,

ATOMIC STEPS

"An imagination is intent to do something about what you've been thinking; a stronghold is when the choice is not yours anymore, but you have submitted your will to the thought."

Imaginations are images, and strongholds are responsible for turning thoughts into reality. Once a thought arrives, the imagination goes to work on it, and if a monopoly is placed on it, that thought becomes reality.

Let's say, for instance, that the thought of stealing comes to mind. It's up to you to dismiss or keep that thought. If you choose to entertain the thought, it will become imagination, or intent to steal. If that thought is caressed, it will evolve into a stronghold and you will end up stealing, unless you submit the temptation to the power of God and, with His help, avoid yielding to it.

You must decide what you're going to do with a thought. Will you discard it, throw it into your recycle bin, or will you employ it? The thoughts you utilize will shape your destiny — either a life of mediocrity or a life of greatness. Evidence of the latter is seen in the lives of Columbus, Copernicus, Gandhi, Winston Churchill, Mother Teresa, Abraham Lincoln, Martin Luther King Jr., Helen Keller, and many others, who, out of their thoughts, accomplished remarkable things. Imagine what would have happened to our civilization if they had discarded those thoughts.

DISCARDED THOUGHTS

"Both poverty and riches are the offspring of thought,"
author Napoleon Hill says in his book *Think and Grow Rich*.

If you're not careful, abandoned thoughts can come back to haunt you. Have you ever given up a thought or idea that came to you, only to later see it achieved by someone else? People frequently tell me they have a great idea for a screenplay. My usual response is, "Why don't you write it or have someone else write it for you?"

But nine times out of 10, they fall asleep on the idea, only to later watch it unfold on the movie screen.

On the other hand, you're constantly bombarded by negative thoughts that, if entertained, will hurt the way you do life. Those thoughts — ones that belittle, dehumanize, and keep you in bondage — are the ones you must change. You must let go of thoughts that tell you that you came from nothing, will never amount to anything, and are no good. "What makes you think you have it in you to accomplish anything worthwhile?" those thoughts say,

ATOMIC STEPS

"You failed yesterday, and you are destined to fail again today."
The truth is nobody has ever accomplished anything worthwhile without changing those kinds of thoughts.

LESSONS FROM MOM

When I was a little boy growing up on the islands of Saint Vincent and the Grenadines, my mom, seemed like she always knew the right thing to say. She would say, very philosophically:
"What you give out in your right hand you're going to receive in your left. You can do whatever you set in your heart and mind to accomplish. If you can think it, you can do it."
For a while, I thought she was too immersed in the Word. But a portion of it did resonate in my delicate mind.
Additionally, she loved painting pictures for all nine of us, by telling stories. I recall this one she told me whenever I lagged in completing my daily chores. I have used it extensively because I feel its application. She told us about Harriet from our village who would go daily down to the river to wash clothes. Harriet would sit on this huge riverstone with the soap and laundry next to her and pray to God that

he would help her wash the daily increasing load of clothes. Well, help never came. She did not even dare to start. Harriet had faith but was not willing to do the work. Consequently, help never came.

About faith it is said:

Faith is the substance of things hoped for, the evidence of things not seen... Faith without works is dead. Therefore, faith can be classified as a belief that is not based on proof.

MOM'S UNDYING LOVE

As a kid, I had the opportunity to see love in action seven out of seven. My mom, though a victim of poor academics, wasted not a single moment working endlessly and tirelessly by day, and nightly encouraging us around a kerosene lamp – back then we didn't have electricity. She wanted all nine of us to be endowed in our chosen calling; opportunities which she never had. With smoke in our eyes, we burned the midnight oil in our effort to excel. When Dad passed on in 1967, a financial reverse began, Mom fought through it and with some of her meager resources saw me through most of high school. I remembered her saying,

"John, this is all I can afford."

ATOMIC STEPS

Despite not having riches and only just enough, along with a busy lifestyle, she found time to open her door to a stranger, neighbor, or friend – providing them with a warm meal while she articulated God's unfailing love. She cared for the sick, and the needy, shared groceries with them and most of all communicated her faith in God. I witnessed many lives changed because she cared. Although we didn't have all the gadgets other kids did back then, she taught us how to share whatever little we had.

Mom's multiple battles with Alzheimer's disease for almost two decades ended in 2005. However, her undying love lives on today and will last for countless generations.

TURNING THOUGHTS INTO REALITY

I was obsessed with becoming a police officer when I grew up, for example, so I studied police officers and prayed to God that someday I would become one. Today, the profession doesn't intrigue me in the same way it used to, but many of the screenplays I've written are about police officers or have something to do with law enforcement. What my mother told me as a child, I've realized, has merit. Thoughts hold magic and power.

ATOMIC STEPS

As a dad, I make it a habit to tell my three sons, now ages 28, 26, and 23, not only that I love them and am proud of them, but also that they can do anything they can imagine. They believe in their ability and, as a result, the two eldest have already embarked upon the task of collaboratively writing their first Disney-type screenplay. They are developing the will to win.

BELIEVE IT, CONCEIVE IT

In *Think and Grow Rich*, Hill talks about a secret hidden in the pages. If you're ready to receive it, he says, you already possess one half; you'll acquire the other half once it reaches your mind. This secret, he adds, cannot be had at any price by those who are not intentionally searching for it. So, I read the book in hot pursuit and with an open mind, believing to conceive. Ideas came to me in abundance, and I juggled them. My favorites? "Your thoughts and desires serve as the magnet which attracts units of life, from the great ocean of life out there." And "All achievement, all earned riches, have their beginning in an idea."

Belief is a powerful force that drives thought. Good thoughts are usually born out of inspiration, and to be inspired, you must be in alignment with God. At one point during Jesus' ministry, His disciples failed to cast a demon out of a little boy; they lacked faith.

ATOMIC STEPS

But Jesus rebuked the demon and he departed from the child.

"Later, the disciples came to Jesus asking, 'Why couldn't we cast him out?' And Jesus said unto them, 'Because of your unbelief: for verily I say unto you, "If you have faith as a mustard seed, you shall say unto this mountain, 'Remove hence to yonder place;' and it shall remove;" and nothing shall be impossible unto you." (Matt. 17:19-20)

In the story of David and Goliath, David's peers probably saw a mountain standing in his way but his faith in the Lord produced an unexpected outcome in battle.

"When Goliath looked at David and saw that he was only a boy, tanned and handsome, he looked down on David with disgust. He said, 'Do you think I am a dog, that you come at me with a stick?' He used his gods' names to curse David; He said to David, 'Come here I'll feed your body to the birds of the air and the wild animals!' But David said unto him, 'You come to me using a sword and two spears. But I come to you in the name of the Lord All-Powerful, the God of the armies of Israel! You have spoken against him." (1 Sam. 17:42-45)

David saw the giant as too big to miss and slew him with a few stones and a slingshot. What giants are standing in your way, daring you to take that next step?

ATOMIC STEPS

Belief inspires one to do the seemingly impossible. An inspired person is apt to break bonds of restraint in his or her mind to accomplish tasks in a record-breaking style.

Through inspiration, Chicago Bulls player Michael Jordan pursued respect for himself and his team by scoring three times his jersey number as he dropped 69 points on the Cleveland Cavaliers in March 1990. Whenever you have an inspired thought, you must trust it and act on it.

THE WILL TO SUCCEED

After the Screen Actors Guild commercial strike in 1998, compounded by the effects of 9/11, I struggled as a commercial actor. Previously I'd had a remarkably successful streak of national television spots, landing nine within 13 months. So off I went searching for ways to make things happen. I wasn't going to allow the industry drought to stop me.

Out of the universe, a hunch nudged me: "Why not become a filmmaker? That's what most successful people in Hollywood do." Multiple acquaintances were already climbing that ladder of success, including producer Mark Burg, who saw something in me that I did not see in myself. Whenever his production was filming something locally, he invited me to experience filmmaking.

ATOMIC STEPS

At the time, I had no experience in filmmaking. So, I frequented his movie sets. I was determined to succeed.

Subsequently, I watched a classic 1970s film I liked so much that I thought about remaking it. For the next three weeks, I made phone calls to find out who held the rights to my intended pet project. When I finally contacted the studio, a woman answered the phone and told me they were not interested in selling the rights to a third party.

That statement didn't sit well with me. You see, my plane had already taken off, the fasten-your-seat-belt signs were already extinguished, and the host was serving the beverage of the day. I composed myself, contacted a writer friend whose script was recently optioned by a major studio, and asked him to assist me in writing my script. He did one of the best things a person can do for another: instead of giving me a fish, he showed me how to fish by sending me guidelines for writing a screenplay. I got busy. My mantra echoed,

"I'll write my own. I'll show them. They'll be begging for my work someday."

My imaginary airplane was swiftly gaining altitude.

The initial draft of that first screenplay was completed within 29 days. Later, I gladly showed one of my scripts to an acquaintance of mine who is a director. He not only told me I was such a novice but also said it was the worst screenplay he had ever seen. That hit home like a ton of bricks, and after a few sleepless nights, I went back to the drafting board. About a year later, he read one of my subsequent action thrillers and remarked,

"You have the knack, guy. Not too many people can do it this way."

If I hadn't coupled belief with thought, my ideas might have been left in the recycle bin.

THOUGHTS LEFT IN THE RECYCLE BIN

John F. Kennedy, the youngest and one of the greatest United States presidents, said this:

"The problems of the world cannot possibly be solved by the skeptics or cynics whose horizons are limited by the obvious realities. We need men who can dream of things that never were."

It should alarm you that the ideas that could beckon a revolution and solve most of the world's problems, including AIDS, cancer, and Alzheimer's disease, may be sitting idle in the recycling bins of people's minds. People who allow their thoughts to sit idle are content with inside-the-box thinking, filled with what I call "the could-have-been syndrome." That's the way millions of people live their lives. They create a worldwide "I don't have what it takes" epidemic; as one of my associates says, they have no guts.

ATOMIC STEPS

Every business, building, highway, school, house, song, screenplay, relationship — everything — begins with a thought.

In the book *The Magic of Thinking Big*, David Schwartz writes,

"Think: 'I can do better.' The best is attainable. There's room for doing everything better. Nothing in the world is being done as well as it could be. And when you think, 'I can do better,' ways to do better will appear." Thinking that way will ignite your creative powers and, like the pent-up flow released from a dam, you will become relentless.

USED THOUGHTS

In his book *The Magic of Believing*, Claude Bristol states, "There never was a period in history when we should study our thoughts more, try to understand them, and learn how to improve our position in life by drawing upon the great source of power that lies within each of us."

How can you tell which thoughts are good and which thoughts are bad? Think of the mind — your storehouse of thoughts — as an empty hard drive in a computer. It knows nothing except what you put into it. The real you are your heart, or your spirit, from where all issues of life flow. I've made it a habit for over a decade to feed my computer – the mind with" good" by reading and listening to inspirational material just before bed. Sometimes I fall asleep while listening. But because my subconscious is still awake while I sleep, it absorbs the bulk of the information. I've noticed that at times throughout the day, inspirational thoughts and messages hit me. And often, when I'm in a situation where it's crucial to find the right words, I'm able to deliver.

Upon acting on the idea to author portions of this book, I felt as if the floodgates of my heart and mind opened, pouring out a storehouse of inspiration. I was directed to previously read books in my library and even to the page, and the highlighted quote, needed for the appropriate insert.

When it comes to thought, only you can determine what is installed on your computer. Remember, input equals output. What you sow you shall also reap.

THINKING OUTSIDE OF THE BOX

Thought largely determines the "haves" from the "have nots" today. Author Victor Hugo said,
"Nothing else in the world ... not all the armies ... is so powerful as an idea whose time has come."
And Warren Bennis, in his book *On Becoming a Leader*, writes,
"A leader is, by definition, an innovator. He does things other people haven't done or don't do. He does

ATOMIC STEPS

things in advance of other people. He makes new things. He makes old things new."

We all can change what we touch for the better, and if we take advantage of our God-given potential, we'll leave this world a better place than we found it. After all, we were formed by the One who created everything; without Him, nothing was made. He loves always and gives bountifully when we serve Him in spirit and truth. If in His image we were formed and molded, why should we profess any form of inhibition? Why do we let small thinking control us? Could it be that we refrain from being plugged into the source — our infinite God? What happens to a river that refuses to draw water from its source?

If we think with a mindset of giving, we entertain abundance, and if we think with an attitude of withholding, we invite lack. The Bible states in Luke 6:38,

"Give, and you will receive. You will be given a lot. Pressed down, shaken together, and running over, it will spill into your lap. The way you give to others is the way God will give to you."

As the source gives to the stream so ought the stream to impart to the ocean.

In 1980, I was greeted by the Statue of Liberty, subway stations, taxis, and massive pedestrian traffic upon my entrance into New York City. A few years before, still living in the Islands, I had seen pictures of the city's

ATOMIC STEPS

greatest landmarks through a viewfinder on loan from a friend. I dreamed of living in the Big Apple, and I finally made it. After years of balancing odd jobs, seeds for my acting career were planted and took root.

My quest for creating started back when I drove taxis there in New York. My yearning to become an actor gnawed at me. One evening I picked up a passenger in Queens on his way to Manhattan, and we struck up a conversation. He said he was an actor and thought I had a great presence and would look powerful on screen. I told him I had been thinking about the possibility of acting for quite some time. Before leaving the cab, he not only gave me the name of his acting school and a contact person but also left his number in case I needed further assistance with my enrollment at Lee Strasberg Institute. The rest is history.

Moving to Los Angeles to pursue an acting career has, in many ways, broadened my horizons, enhanced my thinking, and expanded my vision. My experiences gained from "The University of Hard Knocks" have given me the idea and the drive to write, and today, this book is a result of that seed-planting-fruit-bearing thought.

Claude Bristol states: in The Magic of Believing, "The secret of success lies not without, but within, the thoughts of man."

ATOMIC STEPS

THE POWER OF THOUGHT

Napoleon Hill states in his book *Think and Grow Rich*, "It has been said that man can create anything which he can imagine."

Pascal had this to say:

"Man's greatness lies in his power of thought." Thoughts are magnetic. They will attract people who support them and create an environment in which they can grow, producing after their kind.

You, too, can attract what you want, and the strength of the thought vibration will determine the strength of its attraction. A mere wish lacks the tenacity necessary to get unleashed.

By changing your thoughts, you will change your expressions, and eventually, your world. Everything you accomplish or fail to accomplish in life will be a direct result of the thoughts you cherish in your mind and the words that come out of your mouth. Wherever you are right now, everything you've experienced has prepared you for this moment in time.

Our achievements of today are but the total of our thoughts of yesterday. You are today where the thoughts of yesterday have brought you and will be tomorrow where the thoughts of today take you.
— Pascal

3

CHANGING YOUR WORDS

The power of words and their influence over making things happen goes back to the pre-Eden days. The world was empty without form and darkness covered the ocean.
"Then God said, 'Let there be light,' and there was light." (Gen. 1:2-3) He spoke, and it was done.

YOU GET WHAT YOU SAY

"My brothers and sisters, can a fig tree make olives, or can a grapevine make figs? No! And a well of salty water cannot give good water."

ATOMIC STEPS

James 3:12 confirms.

On and on the list goes. Most kids today suffer from low self-esteem that they didn't create. Kendall White, writing on Youth Motivation states:

"Many of today's youth suffer from negative attitudes and negative environments. Too many of our young people are being raised in environments, which subject them to multiple forms of abuse."

No wonder there are so many unwanted childhood pregnancies and hosts of juvenile detention centers.

Why can't parents tell their children that they're the best — that they love them and are proud of them? Parents usually cherish those sentiments during the embryonic stage, and then at birth and before they begin analyzing the person who has come into their lives. But somewhere along the way, those emotions fade.

Parents need to admit that they're not perfect — that they're a work in progress, too. And kids need to keep on hearing words of affirmation to possess a healthy self-image.

WHAT YOU SAY TO YOUR SPOUSE

Spouses sometimes have a similar problem supporting and building up one another. Instead of voicing love and affirmation, they use phrases such as these:

ATOMIC STEPS

- You're a born loser.

- You're the worst.

- You never do things right.

- I don't know why I married you.

- We've got the worst marriage.

- Everything is wrong with our relationship.

- Your friend is a better husband to his wife.

- You never do the dishes.

- We don't have enough money.

- Our life's a mess.

- You're always late.

- I want a divorce.

No wonder 50% of all first-time marriages end in divorce within an average time of eleven years. Most of them collapse within the first five years. This might not

ATOMIC STEPS

be the case if couples would continue with the great words they uttered during courtship:

- You're the spice of my life.

- There's no me without you.

- It's amazing to watch you grow.

- You make me happy.

- We're a team.

- I love you and I'm proud of you.

- I was wrong; I'm sorry; I apologize.

What an effect this kind of speech could have on our divorce stats!

Words have the same effect on a person's life as gravity on objects in space. If you were to jump freely off the roof of a tall building, you would fall to the ground; there isn't an alternative. Words, too, can cause a person to fall if thought gives way to a reckless decision. But if your mind, the storehouse of your thoughts, is controlled, it becomes easier to control the mouth. And you don't risk facing the inevitable danger of carelessly uttered words. Pro-verbs 13:2-3 says this:

ATOMIC STEPS

"People will be rewarded for what they say, but those who can't be trusted want only violence. Those who are careful about what they say protect their lives, but whoever speaks without thinking will be ruined."

WHAT YOU SAY TO YOURSELF

"The words you have said will be used to judge you." (Matt. 12:37) So many times I run into so-called Christians who give our Creator and their life a bad rap by the words they speak:

- I've got so much bad luck.

- I'm sick.

- I've got no money.

- Nobody loves me.

- I don't have what it takes to succeed.

- I can't stand them. They've got it better than me.

- I've prayed for it and it's just not working out.

ATOMIC STEPS

They forget their tongue is a weapon with the ability to destroy them, the issuer, and the recipient. To guard against someone's reckless speech on your behalf, you must speak your own words of faith. Words of faith attract God's blessing the same way as a magnet draws steel.

"When we put bits into the mouths of horses to make them obey us, we can control their whole bodies. Also, a ship is very big, and it is pushed by strong winds. But a very small rudder controls a big ship, making it go wherever the pilot wants. It is the same with the tongue. It is a small part of the body, but it brags about great things. A big forest fire can be started with a little flame. And the tongue is like fire. It is a whole world of evil among the parts of our bodies. The tongue spreads its evil through the whole body. The tongue is set on fire by hell, and it starts a fire that influences all of life. ... We use our tongues to praise our Lord and Father, but then we curse people, whom God made like himself. My brothers and sisters, this should not happen. Do good and bad water flow from the same spring?" (James 3:2-6, 9-11)

While Proverbs 18:21 states,

"What you say can mean life or death. Those who speak with care will be rewarded."

Words, by the power of the Almighty God, created the universe and the body that you now live in. Your

ATOMIC STEPS

words mixed with faith will propel you toward your destiny.

CHANGING WHAT YOU SAY

Why are words so powerful? Because they govern our hearts and control our physical bodies, steering us toward our desired goals and dreams.

Years ago, my senior pastor's wife was diagnosed with breast cancer. Though our church believes in miracles and the power of prayer, we watched her fight this disease with the power of words. I saw her a few times during her travail and found out that she carried around index cards with words of confession and affirmation; she didn't want anything to do with the sometimes fatal disease. Prayers were poured out on her behalf, and it's believed that she confessed her healing. Today, she travels all over the world teaching people the power of the Word over sickness in the body. You cannot speak both sickness and disease and expect to

walk in good health.

What would your life be like if you were to use these motivating faith-filled words?

- No weapon formed against me shall prosper.

ATOMIC STEPS

- "I can do all things through Christ which strengthened me." (Phil. 4:13 KJV)

- "The steps of a good man are ordered by the Lord." (Ps. 37:23 KJV)

- I refuse to renounce my self-image, no matter what happens to me.

To paraphrase my favorite inspirational one-liners from Bishop T.D. Jakes messages:

- The battle is not mine; it belongs to the Lord.

- What God has for me no devil in hell can take.

- I was born to do this.

- The time has come for my change.

- God is taking me where no man has gone before.

- I must prosper.

- I can have what God says I can have.

ATOMIC STEPS

- I will rise! I will finish.

- When it's all said and done, I'll come out of it.

- I'm the head and not the tail.

- You may whip some but not me. I'm going to force you to give up.

- I have what it takes for my dream.

- I'm a giant killer.

- I'm chosen. I can take less and do more with it.

- God wants me to be so blessed that I live in the land of much.

- God is opening doors for me that no man can shut.

What a difference it will make in your Climb if, as the flood storms of life come against you, you riveted keep climbing.

You ought to not just speak your desires but must also believe that what you say will happen. If you cultivate bad thoughts, the words you speak will, like the fruit of a poisoned vine, destroy you. As thought seeds grow

ATOMIC STEPS

through your spoken words, so will the change within you.

No longer will you step aside to let Crusaders go by. Others will step aside for you because you are now a crusader.
— William Danforth

4

CHANGING YOUR ACTIONS

You possess a great and powerful asset that, if utilized, will lift you to insurmountable heights in your life. The things that others call impossible will be yours for the taking. This asset I mention will not only bring you confidence but will also give you total satisfaction and peace of mind.

You possess the power to change. Once you recognize that power and learn how to use it, changes in the way you act will be automatic. You'll become like a butterfly that has left its cocoon; your thoughts and words will have

ATOMIC STEPS

transformed you and you will be ready to act. You will have purpose and direction in your life. You will have said goodbye to indecision and welcomed success and prosperity into your life, blessing the lives of others in the process.

Your decisions influence how you will live the remainder of your life. Choice precedes action as day precedes night. Life moves swiftly, and you need to act before you're acted upon.

What positive actions are you willing to take? How strong is your courage? Do you want what you touch to turn to gold? Is there a thought seed you've sown with words of faith that you're now ready to prune and watch bear fruit? Are you ready to take some action?

Most people are content to sit back and wait for things to come to them. They're going through life waiting for their ships to come in when they've never even set sail. You may have all the talent in the world, but if you're hiding your light under a bushel, the world won't know it. You will only attract the world by going to it with your shining light. The world must know that you exist.

TOMORROW PEOPLE

"Tomorrow People" are those who prefer to wait for their world to come to them instead of meeting it head-on. They will tell you that they are going to get started tomorrow. The problem is that tomorrow turns into another tomorrow, and then another tomorrow, and another, and so on. Talent does not guarantee success. It's what you do with the talent that counts. When you move toward your world, your world moves toward you.

What limitations are you placing on yourself? Wouldn't you rather try to succeed and fail than do nothing at all? Are you waiting for tomorrow?

Some people like to watch things happen, some people like to wait for things to happen, some people like to wonder what will happen, and some people don't care what happens. But the action-driven person delights in making things happen. Keith DeGreen states in Creating a Success Environment,

"Yesterday is a canceled check; tomorrow is a promissory note."

If it's going to happen, it's up to you to strike that spark. Some people create, while others compete. Creating is where the rubber meets the road. A dream worth having is one worth fighting for because freedom is not free; it carries a massive price tag.

Let me reiterate this classic story: When I was a kid, my mom told me a story about a woman who would take her laundry to the river every day, sit

ATOMIC STEPS

down on a huge stone with the soap and laundry next to her, and pray to God that he'd send her help to wash the daily-increasing load. But help never came. She might have had faith, but she wasn't willing to do the work, and help never came. What are you willing to do with the gifts and abilities that have been given to you? Is your dare strong enough to cause you to swim upstream when others around you are content to float downstream?

"Every fish that swims upstream is worth ten that loaf in lazy bays,"

William Danforth says in his book I Dare You.

I've seen so many people who just sit on their talent. They have no zest, vim, vitality, passion, or sense of purpose. Nothing drives them. They are like a train without an engine. And they wonder why others are moving ahead in life while they're not. They're waiting for someone to inject them with a dose of success or, like the woman with the laundry, praying that God will bless their idle deeds.

BECOME A CRUSADER

In his book, Danforth also writes this challenge: "I am looking for you, one of the audacious few, who will face life courageously, ready to strike at the heart of anything that is keeping you from your best; you intrepid ones behind whom the world moves forward."

Additionally, he tells a story about a young man who was working as a secondhand on a railroad. The man's thoroughness had won him an opportunity to work for a few days in a shipping office. During the interim, the superintendent asked this young substitute clerk for some vital data. The young man didn't know anything about bookkeeping, but he worked three days and three nights without sleep and had the facts ready for the superintendent when he returned. That act of decision and commitment later propelled him into the vice-presidency seat of his own company.

A few years ago, I worked as a property manager for a residential complex. One of my tenants was a young producer who had just gone through a disheartening divorce. My three young boys and I had the chance to spend some time with him and his 3-year-old son, and I realized during our visits that he spent most of his time reading movie scripts. An associate of mine told me that one day, he saw him on an airplane with at least six scripts in his briefcase. Today, he's not only engaged to a great woman, but he's also one of the most successful independent film producers in Hollywood and owns a movie franchise that has

ATOMIC STEPS

grossed over $100 million a year for the past three years. He's what I call a true crusader.

Once you acquire the action habit, others have no choice but to step aside for you; you're a crusader, and the world always seems to make way for the person who knows where he's going. Even traffic on crowded streets makes way for a fire engine on a mission. Take one step forward and your enemies will run for cover.

CHART YOUR COURSE

Action cures fear. Become known for doing things. When you see something that you believe ought to be done, step up to the plate and hit a home run. Don't wait for conditions to be perfect. They never will. The losers in life always wait for an invitation to succeed. You have the right to be uncommon as you set and reach for your goals — and a life of which you can be proud. Former President Theodore Roosevelt stated:

"I choose not to be a common man. Me, it's my right to be uncommon if I can. I'll seek opportunity, not security. I do not wish to be a kept citizen — humbled and dulled by having the state look after me. I want to take calculated risks, to dream and to build, to fail and to succeed. I'll refuse to live from hand to mouth. I prefer the challenges of life to the

ATOMIC STEPS

Most of our potential lies dormant in us because:

1. We fail to realize that we are blessed beyond measure.
2. We succumb to the effects of loss, guilt, heartbrokenness, low self-esteem, and under-appreciativeness for far too long.
3. Fear the four-letter word, described as **F**alse **E**vidence **A**ppearing **R**eal; blocks us from becoming the best we can be.

How many times have you said **no** to your potential? How many times have you **stared** at a terrific opportunity in the face and said no to yourself because of your past defeats? How many times has someone told you that you can't do something or can't do all you were created to be? Most of us carry around too much junk in the trunk. The things that you and others call impossible will be yours for the taking if you eliminate that junk and choose to act.

Action is a *doing* word! Once you acquire this habit, others have no choice but to step aside for you. You are now a crusader, and the

ATOMIC STEPS

world always seems to make way for the person who knows where he or she is going. Look at a fire engine, mission-bound, speeding up your street.

In Los Angeles, California it is a rule, whenever a fire engine is in pursuit – everything gives way. Despite how desperate the drivers of those now parked vehicles are, towards arriving at their destinations. Also, I have witnessed dogs barking at these passion-ate, purpose-driven pursuits of a fire engine. Never once have I seen any fire engine stop to address them. Could those dogs be saying in their language?

"You are going too fast and making too much noise. No one can keep up, not even me. You need to slow down; don't you hear me? I am barking for you to slow down. Are you deaf?"

How about those people who are content to consistently sit on their good intentions? Sitting there is one of the major causes of failure. Lackadaisically, they allow opportunities to pass them by. They lack zest, vim, vitality as well as the ability to swim upstream and associate with others who are content with floating downstream.

ATOMIC STEPS

They operate their lives like a train without an engine. Then when others around them are moving ahead they become envious, wishing that these action-driven individuals never succeed at their chosen vocation. Failure to act, a fear epidemic paralyzing many would-be champions in our world has a simple cure. It's action. The people who act on their ideas are not only successful but, in most cases, amass great fortunes.

Some people watch things happen, some people like to wait for things to happen, some people like to wonder what will happen, and some people don't care what happens, but the action-driven person delights in making things happen. Give a task to a busy person and they finish it speedily. Watch them go to work on it and you will notice how their actions exude confidence. He's bound to succeed.

On the other hand, many are known to wait for their ship to come in when it has not even left the dock.

"Oh, if I could just get lucky like you the ambitious person" they whine. "Oh, if only I had your lucky breaks."

Give your lucky breaks to them and watch them crumble. Why? Your shoes are not only

ATOMIC STEPS

uncomfortable but too big for them. They have not seen the sacrifices you have made as you keep discerning your disappointments daily, to gain the stripes on your lapel or the gold medal around your neck.

What actions are you hesitant to take, knowing that by acting, your life would turn around for the better? What if the life you've always envisioned, could be heading your way today if you were to step out and meet it halfway? What actions are holding you back? Good things come to those who are filled with passion and purpose and launch out into the deep; not to those who sit back and wait.

Years ago, I was at a business conference on the East Coast and heard the keynote speaker share this story:

A very wealthy man bought a huge ranch in Arizona and invited some of his closest associates to see it. After touring the 1,500 acres of mountains, rivers, and grasslands, he took everybody to the house. The house was as spectacular as the scenery. In the back of the house was the largest swimming pool they had ever seen. However, it was filled with alligators. The owner explained:

ATOMIC STEPS

"I value courage more than anything. It is what made me a billionaire. I value courage so much that if anyone dares to jump in that pool and swim to the other side, I will give them whatever they want, my land, my house, my money, anything."

Of course, everybody laughed at the challenge and turned to follow the owner into the house for lunch. Suddenly they heard a splash. Turning around they saw a guy splashing and thrashing into the water, swimming for his life as the alligators swarmed after him. After multiple death-defying seconds, the man made it unharmed to the other side. The rich billionaire was amazed but he stuck to his promise.

He said,

"You are a man of courage, you can have anything you want, house, money, land, whatever you want is yours."

The swimmer, breathing heavily, looked up and said,

"I just want to know who pushed me in the pool."

-Unknown

ATOMIC STEPS

Some examples of being pushed into action include the story of one Alabama sewer: One December evening in 1955, a seamstress for a department store in Montgomery, Alabama boarded a city bus en route to her home. It was during the civil rights revolution when blacks were only legally permitted to sit at the back of a bus. She walked past the "whites only" section towards the middle of the bus. With frequent stops, the bus filled up. The driver, a white man, noticed that more people of his race were still boarding. So, he ordered the people in the seamstress Rosa Parks' row to move to the back of the bus. They gave him a deaf ear. Frustrated, he barked at those black passengers. They all moved to the back except for Rosa Parks. Consequently, she was arrested and sent to jail after a sheriff was called to the scene.

Parks' enthusiastic act fueled the already simmering civil rights movement with Martin Luther King at the helm. Today in America, not only are Black people and other minorities permitted to vote but, a Black man recently sat in the White House as our commander and chief. Being pushed seems to bring out the best in most people, enabling them to use more of their potential.

ATOMIC STEPS

Less than a decade ago, I was driven to write. I never envisioned myself being a writer; frankly, it was the furthest vocation from my mind.

In 1994, I attended Lee Strasburg Institute in New York and subsequently launched my acting career. I instantly fell in love with the craft. After multiple Off-Broadway engagements, incorporating performances at the famous *Paper Mill Playhouse* in New Jersey, I brought my skill to Hollywood in 1996.

A few years later, several feature films as well as several national TV campaigns were under my belt. As I stated in my book, **When The Dust Settles** *(A True Hollywood Story)*, I was forced into writing or to put it more subtly, it became a blessing in disguise.

While operating a modeling agency and almost going bankrupt in 2004, I stumbled into a 1970s classic film, which I so badly wanted to remake. At the time, I had no prior experience in filmmaking, except for my previous time spent on movie sets. Nonetheless, I was determined to write. I knew exactly how I wanted to remake this project.

For the next three weeks, I made multiple phone calls to find out who held the rights to my intended pet project. When I finally contacted the studio, a woman answered the phone and told me they were not interested in selling the rights to a third party.

ATOMIC STEPS

That statement didn't sit well with me. You see, concisely - my plane had already taken off, the fasten-your-seat-belt signs were already extinguished, and the hostess was serving the beverage of the day. Flying was inevitable.

So, I composed myself, contacted a writer friend whose script was recently optioned by a major studio, and asked him to assist me in writing my script. He did one of the best things a person can do for another. Instead of giving me a fish, he showed me how to fish by sending me guidelines for writing a screenplay. I got busy writing. My mantra echoed for months,

"I'll write my own. I'll show them. They'll be begging for my work someday."

My imaginary airplane was swiftly gaining altitude.

I knew "if it was going to be" it was up to me! I knew where I came from and where I wanted to go. At this point, I took inventory of myself and *concluded that the individual who was born in St. Vincent and the Grenadines and grew up in poverty was determined to turn his world around.* What I touched had to turn to gold. I Dared the ones who tried to get in my way. After my debut, in writing screenplays, I experienced a supernatural divine encounter.

ATOMIC STEPS

One day, while sitting at my desktop computer, pondering my next steps, I was led to study the life of Dr. Martin Luther King and all that he represented. He had always been my hero. I stared at his picture intermittently for several days. At that point, I was thirsty to write my first book. I knew that I cataloged incredibly unique stories to share.

So, on January 21st, 2007, after having a heart-to-heart, mind-over-matter interlude with my hero, hidden guide, and mentor MLK Jr., I took that leap of faith or to put it more subtly – I took the first step. Reflecting on what Dr. King stood for, I reasoned: If only I could do 20 % of what he stood for, I would be incredibly happy and, in the process, advance civilization.

So, I committed my time, skill, and resources to writing consistently. In the spring of 2007, my first book, *The 5 Steps to Changing Your Life* was written. With writing skills well below par, (writing as a one-finger typist) I completed the first draft of that book 84 pages in one week. I felt as if a dam of inspiration had flooded through my mind, as I paced back and forth from my computer to my book library. I perused through my book collection, including *The Magic of Thinking Big*, a book I read for the first time over twenty years ago. In those books, I found the necessary highlighted

ATOMIC STEPS

quotes, which I needed to insert into my manuscript. I devoured the book: I Dare You: By William Danforth. While the editor worked on the book, I created the outline for my next book. It turned out to be the by-product of that inspirational deluge.

Writing my first book not only caused me to tap into my unused potential but also brought me off the sidelines and into the game. I was ready to hustle, shake, and bake. No one was going to outwork me. Since I had never taken a typing class, I was not adept at using the computer's keyboard. My word per minute was about a few words a minute. Someone once said: *When the dream is big enough the facts don't count.*

In the summer of 2008, I wrote, published, and released my second book - **Spread Some Love (Relationships 101)**. I believe that if my thoughts can produce it, it can be written. To date, I have authored more than 75 books in print, with additional works in progress.

In hindsight, I was pushed into writing. I was heaved into action toward my calling, (a blessing in disguise) after being denied access to *that movie's rights*. The company probably meant it for evil, but God meant it for good. Therefore, deciding to swim upstream was non-negotiable. In the words of Poet Robert Frost:

"The woods are lovely, dark, and deep. But I have promises to keep and miles to go before I sleep."

Champions are action-driven, stroke after stroke, play after play, day after day, even if it seems like nothing is happening. Like a duck's feet moving underwater, they are mentally or physically working on their game. You may not see it on the outside, but it happens inside of them. The roots of a giant oak tree are submerged deep below the ground. Yes, that massive oak that withstands the wind and rain. It is as strong above the ground as it is below the ground. Its roots submerge because of simple mundane actions to support that winning tree.

How do you want to be counted? Danforth further challenges:

"Are you content to have posterity look at your life so far and say, 'That is all he was capable of?' Or are you one of the priceless few, one of those with a restless feeling that someday you are going to climb to your rightful place of leadership? That someday you are going to create something worthy of your best?"

As you change your thoughts, you will change your words, your actions, your character, and

ATOMIC STEPS

other characteristics, you will eventually step off the bench, into the game, and WIN!

According to J. R. Miller, *The only thing that walks back from the tomb with the mourners and refuses to be buried is the character of a man.*

Our deepest fear is not that we are inadequate.
Our deepest fear is that we are powerful beyond measure.
It is our light, not our darkness that most frightens us.

We ask ourselves, who am I to be brilliant, gorgeous, talented, and fabulous?
Actually, who are you not to be?
You are a child of god. Your playing small doesn't serve the world.

There's nothing enlightened about shrinking so that other people won't feel insecure around you.
We were born to make manifest the glory of God that is within us.
It's not just in some of us, it's in everyone.

And, as we let our light shine, we unconsciously permit other people to do the same. As we are liberated from our fear, our presence automatically liberates others.

- Marianne Williamson

5

BREAKING FREE

In his book, The Genius Machine author Gerald Sindell asks:
"How can you get out of your ocean to see what differentiates you?"
Based on the world's populace of almost seven billion people, you stand out. You might reason – Really? Me? That's impossible. I am nobody. I don't have a brain. I am from the wrong side of the tracks I don't have what it takes. I am not the best tool in the shed. I am not. I am not, and I am not. If you are holding onto those false beliefs about yourself – Understand, that they are

ATOMIC STEPS

nothing but figments of your imagination. Whenever you view any album of photographs or a photo album, there's that human tendency to look double to see if you are included in those pictures, you look initially for yourself, even if you were not part of the photo shoot. Furthermore, if you were to, with time permitting check out the entire world's population, you won't find anyone exactly like you, including anyone with your peculiar abilities, intelligence, or viewpoint. Have you ever pondered and realized that there's a reason you are the only one with your voice, thumbprint along with many other attributes?

You may not believe it, comprehend it, or even decipher it. Even so, if I were to tell you that you have the power within you to become successful: **A force that is at this moment in time, dormant.** When discovered and aroused, it will lift you from failure to success - A power that will dramatically transform you into a person of tremendous influence and success. And what if I were to tell you that all you must do was to trust your power by knowing yourself? In his book On Becoming a Leader Warren Bennis writes: Know thyself, then, means separating who you are and who you want to be from what the world thinks you are and wants you to be. It is often said that

ATOMIC STEPS

"knowledge is power." Self-knowledge subsequently is your first key to success. See, if you seriously, I propose, genuinely get acquainted with you, and understand that the sky is the limit to your potential, you may not be able to go to sleep tonight. Captivated by such a burning desire to tap into that 90% unused potential that remains unleashed, you'd be wide awake planning the next series of moves for your life.

In addition, if I were to tell you that by believing in yourself, breaking old failure habits, changing your negative associates who've been constantly holding you back, and developing a sense of passion and purpose toward fulfilling your destiny. Would you, in exchange for a better, fuller, and richer life, step up to the plate?

YOU must realize that you're different. You are unique. You are beautiful and wonderfully made. When God made you, he destroyed the formula. He must have jubilantly said to his angels "There can never be another you! Some may try to imitate you, but it's a futile battle. You can never, never, be recreated." You are here, right now, and no one can be you but you. Be excitingly thankful for who you are as well as who you can become. Imagine what would have happened if your

ATOMIC STEPS

mom had swung a little to her left or your dad had swung a little to his right. Result? - Missed target. Someone besides you eventually would have made it to this world. Those million-plus tiny sperm cells racing through that dark alley to impregnate that patiently waiting egg, would have eagerly decided someone else's conception. Unfortunately, and tragically, as human beings we place extraordinarily little value on ourselves and subsequently acclimatize toward failure. We live in a world bombarded with negative news, pessimism, and a failure mindset. As a result, devaluing ourselves has become such an easy thing to do. Watching Constant Negative News for a few hours over a period we are hooked, immersed in all that negativity. As the saying goes, "garbage in garbage out." You hear and watch so much violence, now you're even afraid to go outside. Besides, you've not merely become fearful of others, but also you fear your potential. This results in living your life with your light hidden under a bushel.

As a responsible individual on your way to the top, realize that you are always looking at two different walls. You'll find that one says you are top-notch, and you can do whatever you can think, want, or desire. The other says: You have no capital. You are uneducated. You don't have the energy it takes. You have failed before. You are too old. You are too young. You lack talent and abilities. You are too short, too tall. Too - everything. You are too ill-equipped to succeed in life.

Conversely, when it comes down to causing a change, everything starts with you. You are in the driver's seat. You are in charge. You are the captain of your rowboat. You are the pilot of your aircraft. You set your own pace. Most of all you are the only handicap you must encounter towards your destiny. You chose success or failure – both learned vocations. The ball is in your hands – you dribble, or you shoot. When it all comes down to it if you miss, there's no one else to blame.

Any individual bent on success must eliminate the blame game from his or her mindset to have success. He focuses on his destiny. By doing so he develops the morale that "It's all or nothing." He eats, lives, and breathes successfully. Thereby - creating war on any vice, which has kept or will keep him captive. With such a mindset, stepping out of his comfort zone becomes an embracing challenge. Consequently, this move results in a much richer and more rewarding lifestyle. In my book When the Dust Settles - I am still standing. I referred to the story about the baby elephant

ATOMIC STEPS

chained to a stake, and years later, with the chain removed from its feet, conversely that elephant refused to set itself free. Living such a life tied to our circumstances - is a shell we must crack if our advancing is going to be inevitable.

Breaking free and being all, you care about will take effort. I am always reminded of the story of two men waiting at the dock. One man looked like he had been waiting there forever, putrid, and unkempt, smoking a cigarette. A ship pulled up and dropped that huge piece of iron to anchor. An agile man boarded, and while doing so, glanced at the dormant man, and remarked, "Good to see you again, pal." Then he jumped aboard the ship. Before setting sail, he asked the waiting man:

"What are you waiting for friend? I see you here all the time…"

The man responded:

"My ship, of course."

As he lit up another cigarette continuing his chain-smoking interlude. The man on the now sailing ship retorted,

"Did you send one out?"

"No,"

he replied as he took a brisk puff on his cigarette releasing ash.

"Sorry, you have to send one out."

ATOMIC STEPS

the present is pointing to those who have gone before you."

Success is a journey. Though some like to think it's a destination. The people who continue to succeed value themselves and therefore, are not satisfied with who they are. They are constantly changing and enhancing their self-image. They feel as though they have not scratched the surface in their chosen endeavor. They realize that success is all about the hustle and dare anyone to outwork them. In essence, their life must be a worthwhile endeavor. That championship, the Super Bowl, the bestseller, the Oscar, the crowd's approval, the gold medal, the one million church members in attendance, and receiving of the Nobel Prize. Those are all great accomplishments, yet those high achievers are not at all satisfied. They see the world as if it's a complex jigsaw puzzle, and they are the missing piece of the solution. They think,

"If it's going to be fixed - it's up to me."

It doesn't matter who you are, where you are, where you live, what you have or don't have, who your parents are. If you dare to cause that change, you have enlisted yourself in a great cause that will certainly bless humanity beyond your imagination.

ATOMIC STEPS

YOU no doubt by reading this far had already defined yourself. If you are not ready for your success, feel free to pass this volume on to someone else who desires all they have ever wanted to become. However, if you have a burning desire to go through the wall standing in your way for far too long? If you care, enough to succeed massively - your SUCCESS is inevitable!

6

PREPAREDNESS

Preparation is paramount in any undertaking, and when you understand its importance, and move towards your goal and desires, your goals and desires move tenaciously toward you. It is a given that, no man can stop a man with a plan, because no one has the plan to stop him. So, plan your work and work your plan.

Preparation is foundational, that's why it should start with baby steps. Watch any kid walking for the first time or watch a bodybuilder working out for the first time, or any athlete honing his skill. It's mundane, isn't it? Step by step, layer by layer, task by task, these mundane chores are repeated.

ATOMIC STEPS

Doing the mundane is not always comfortable. We often complain about how boring it is to do the same thing repeatedly. Yet, we find that champions do the same things repeatedly to win a championship. They become adept at mastering the mundane.

Michael Phelps, winner of several gold medals during the 2009 Olympics made it a habit of working out in the pool for 8 hours a day for several years to accomplish Olympic distinction. It was said that "One component of Michael Phelps' phenomenal success is his "made-for-swimming" physique. But the main component is the carefully crafted training program that his coach, Bob Bowman, has created for him." Let's notice his journey to Olympic excellence as described by Bowman:

Here, Coach Bowman 2001 ASCA Coach of the Year describes his training protocols and provides sample workouts.

I think it was pretty clear from the beginning that Michael Phelps was a special swimmer. When he joined us at North Baltimore Aquatic Club as a 7-year-old, he was a baseball/ soccer/ lacrosse athlete.

In his first year, he just did a 60-minute, once-a-week stroke clinic with our aquatic director, Cathy Lears. His training and intensity escalated from there to where, by the time he was 10 and setting NAG records, he was

ATOMIC STEPS

better than many of the older swimmers.

We had to do some rapid lane promotions. To those who knew Phelps' aquatic heritage, his prowess was no surprise. His oldest sister, Hilary, was a national-level swimmer. His second sister, Whitney, was also a 200 flyer. She made the 1994 World Championship team that competed in Rome, and she still holds the 11 - 12 NAG record in the 100-yard fly.

So, in many ways, swimming excellence has been a family trait. While it is also tempting to think of Michael only in terms of the fly and IM, a review of his record reveals a litany of national rankings in the free and back as well.

Supportive parents have aided his climb immensely. They had been through the drill with the older daughters.

Then there's Michael's physique: at 6-4, he is mostly torso with a large chest and long arms. It's a body great for swimming. He is very flexible throughout the shoulders, upper body, and especially in the ankles.

Michael is much more disciplined than he was in his earlier days. He was, and still is, a pretty strong-willed kid. Back then, he didn't understand he might have to do some things he didn't want to do, like train, sit still, pay attention, and not talk. He was very energetic as a young boy.

These days, he's modified his behavior- either voluntarily or involuntarily. I think part of that modification started when I pulled him out of the pool

ATOMIC STEPS

and told him, "You've got a stroke that is going to set a world record someday, and you are going to do it in practice."

Michael has an athletic mentality second to none. He is keenly competitive, and that's what drives him. In competition, he is incredibly focused and able to relax. The higher the level of competition, the better he is. That's something you just don't see very often.

What he needs to work on is the same thing he had to work on as a child: to strengthen the connection in his mind between what happens daily and how that affects what's going to happen when he gets to the big meet. He's better now and better than 90 percent of the population, but he still has those days about once every six weeks when he's tired, and it's a struggle for me to get him to do things and maintain the same intensity in workouts that he gives in the big meets.

In 2002, he had an excellent summer, setting a world record in the 400-meter IM, taking four events at the Phillips 66 Summer Nationals, notching American records in the 200 IM and 100 fly, and swimming the fastest fly leg ever in a 4 x 100 world record medley relay victory.

In addition to water work, we religiously incorporated a "Mike Barrowman medicine ball routine" into his dryland routine, and we did a three-week stay at altitude in Colorado Springs. He's followed his long course success with the best fall and winter he's ever had by far.

ATOMIC STEPS

Typically, for the last three or four years, Michael has had very good summers. Then there have been down periods in the fall where we've had to work hard to crank him back up to a good mental mode. That has not been the case this year.

This fall and winter, Michael has worked hard on the backstroke. He's gotten really good. Recently, he finished a 15 x 200-yard back set with a 1:45. Not too bad! And his breaststroke, while still not flashy, is greatly improved.

We continue to develop Michael as a complete swimmer. That means some emphasis on the distance freestyle. On Halloween, he whipped off a 5,000 free for a time in 46:34. That's under a 9:20 per 1,000 average. I was impressed with that. It is probably the most impressive thing he's done, and it might be one of the most impressive things he ever does. That's the kind of thing I'm not sure you can ever replicate, but it's neat to give him some confidence, particularly since he has to swim against some of the super-distance guys.

This is the third year we have approached the training cycle from a yearly perspective. It's not our style at NBAC to talk about the results of success. We are always interested in the process. Michael didn't understand the scope of it until his breakout spring national performance in Seattle in 2000 when he went from a 2:04.68 to 1:59 flat and set a 15-16 NAG record in the 200-meter fly. After that, the secret was out.

ATOMIC STEPS

Michael Phelps was not only told he had a stroke that would set a world record one day, but he needed to prepare himself by doing that stroke in practice. Yes, over, and over, lap after lap, though at times mundane. Simple disciplinary actions, perfected over time, brought him Olympic excellence. Additionally, he was instructed on the need to condition himself like he did as a child, by strengthening the connection in his mind. Phelps learned that what happens daily would affect what happens in the championship. It was imperative to maintain that intensity. So many get caught up in the results, and they forget about the activity necessary to produce those results.

Phelps's appearance at the 2008 Olympics had much to do with his preparedness and his commitment. It has become known that his training intensified, leading up to this moment. Many had never heard of Phelps until his Olympic brilliance as he shocked the world with his performances.

When it comes down to winning the championship, preparedness is a known requirement. If you fail to prepare, you've prepared to fail. I recount the preparedness of one of the greatest failures in history. He was quoted as saying,

"Give me six hours to chop down a tree and I'll

ATOMIC STEPS

spend the first four sharpening the axe."

He failed in business in 1831, he was defeated for the legislature in '32, he was elected to the legislature in '34, his sweetheart died in '35, he had a nervous breakdown in '36, he was defeated for Speaker in '38, he was defeated for elector in '40, he was defeated for Congress in '43, he was elected to Congress in '48, he was defeated for the Senate in '50, and he was defeated for Vice President in '56 and for the Senate in '58. But in 1860, he was elected President of the United States.

His multiple failures prepared him to hold the highest office in our nation. *As President, he built the Republican Party into a strong national organization. Further, he rallied most of the northern Democrats to the Union cause. On January 1, 1863, he issued the Emancipation Proclamation that declared forever free those slaves within the Confederacy.*

Being prepared is a requirement for anyone attempting to win in any chosen endeavor.

7
BELIEF

One of the greatest acts of Belief was displayed by the Man who walked on water. When Jesus walked on this earth it was said he performed multiple miracles. He became the master of taking people from not having to have. He cleansed the person with leprosy, gave sight to the blind, fed the multitudes, restored a severed ear, calmed the stormy sea, walked on water, turned water into wine, and many more. Spectators and recipients saw this amazing power called belief at work firsthand.

ATOMIC STEPS

The power of belief has also moved many individuals from the status of a nobody to a person of not only amazing success but true significance. It has also cured many individuals of fatal diseases, including cancer, as in the case of my pastor's wife. Belief is like a bridge that takes one from not having to have.

Though this imaginary bridge exists, many still lack the inspiration necessary to see beyond their present circumstances. Seeing beyond the horizon seems to be a foe instead of a friend urging them on. Additionally, their actions of yesterday tend to not only bring them to where they are now but also like taking a permanent pit stop. Thus, these actions keep them stuck, because like driving a car, they look in the rearview mirror versus the windscreen. Those same "wanna-be's" will tell you that they would do something to enhance their life "*but*." Thus, their too many "buts" only aid in keeping them where they are versus where they can be.

Believing in yourself has much to do with the value you place on your potential. If you see yourself as "a nobody" that's what you will believe about yourself. Just like the saying

ATOMIC STEPS

goes, "garbage in garbage out" you will receive little instead of much.

I call these believers in you "ladder holders." They wait, holding up the ladder, cheering you on to amazing success. They are looking for people who are willing to make that first step and the second and the third. In you, they recognize not only your amazing potential but your powerful belief. This attraction keeps them standing in the gap, holding onto the ladder until they arrive at the last rung.

A person of value also believes that he or she is among the best, therefore they act and perform at their best. They believe that they can remove mountains therefore they do so. Watch someone who is striving to become all they can be, and you will notice that instead of becoming less, they grow as a person because they are constantly working on themselves. They don't look for things to become easier, instead, they acquire the skills necessary to solve problems as they arise. They know that they are either in the middle of a problem, coming out of a problem, or getting ready to be faced with the next problem. Place a challenge in their path and watch it dissipate. Since they

ATOMIC STEPS

believe that they are resourceful they dominate as an analytical person.

Belief is very powerful; it can drive your thoughts. Believing that something is possible always triggers the mind to find a possible solution.

This reminds me of the story of David in Goliath in the Old Testament. David was matched up against this Philistine giant, who dared David to approach him. His peers probably saw a mountain in his way. David only saw Goliath as too big to miss. Because of this giant-sized faith in God, he slew the giant with a few stones and a slingshot.

What giants are standing in your way right now? Who or what is in your corner telling you that they can't be slain? Do **you** believe they can be slain? Or do you never see an end in sight? Belief, genuine belief, inspires one to do the impossible. Belief causes an individual to break bonds of restraint in his or her mind, to accomplish tasks in record-breaking style. They become resilient, inspired, and unstoppable!

I love sports. Not only are sports exciting to watch. Sports always bring out the combative-ness in athletes. Michael Jordan, one of the greatest players to ever play the

ATOMIC STEPS

game of basketball, displayed tremendous belief in himself. In 1990, while playing for the Chicago Bulls, his inspiration helped him score three times his jersey number by dropping 69 points against the Cleveland Cavaliers.

To become successful at anything, you first must believe that you can. Wishing will never put you in the driver's seat. Most often your belief can be stretched out like the waiting process involved in the growth of a Chinese Bamboo Tree. Understanding the growth process of this unique tree will certainly dispel those doubts and fears that you hold about yourself - those imaginary walls deterring you from ever becoming who you were always meant to be. In my opinion, this is a classic example of doubt and faith put to the test:

You take a little seed and plant, water, and fertilize it for a whole year, and nothing happens.

The second year you water and fertilize it, and nothing happens.

The third year you water and fertilize it, and nothing yet.

The fourth year you water and fertilize it, and still nothing.

ATOMIC STEPS

The fifth year you continue to water and fertilize the seed. Sometime during the fifth year, the Chinese bamboo tree sprouts and grows NINETY FEET IN SIX WEEKS.

This power, based on your deep-rooted feelings about yourself, will harness your resolve and take you to insurmountable heights in your life and career. If you trust it, it will take you from the impossible to amazing success.

All things are possible to him who believes.
Mark 9:23.

If you have genuine faith, described as *"the substance of things hoped for, and the evidence of things not seen"* which embodies belief - in yourself and the process. You are like a bodybuilder developing a robust body. You are ripped! Now let's get ready to step into this next step.

8

MOMENTUM

It has been said that this essential success ingredient is hard to acquire and very easy to lose. "It is not of importance where we stand, but in what direction we are moving," is a known fact. This explains why so many are unable to hold on to their winning ways. Vince Lombardi said:
Winning is a habit, and so is losing.
It takes momentum to win, and momentum comes through growth.
Momentum is not easily acquired because **Preparedness + Action + Belief = Momentum** ®. Those components must be involved in the equation for success to materialize. Momentum also has much

ATOMIC STEPS

to do with synchronicity. The acronym P.A. B® (Preparedness-Action-Belief), must exist to get the big "Mo" which is momentum. Most people unwilling to put the wood in the stove to get heat miss the PAB process and get eluded by the miraculous. I'm sure you've discovered when you are coordinated, things just seem to come to you. You can almost walk on water. In football, you catch that difficult interception. In basketball, you get an unintended pass, a rebound, or a layup. It's like leaping and a net appears. Some say it's a matter of being at the right place at the right time. If we all were *there,* what a mess that would be. We would all be fighting for the same opportunity.

Momentum will ultimately carry one from being ordinary to being extraordinary. Michael Phelps did not just wake up one day and win multiple gold medals. He prepared for over eight years, he then performed repeatedly for years, and when he added his belief to the mix it was said that "he accomplished Olympic excellence."

In 2009, during game 2 of the Eastern Conference NBA finals between The Orlando Magic and The Cleveland Cavaliers, Lebron James of the Cavaliers shot a 3-point buzzer-beater from the top of the key almost 23 feet from the basket. His team won the game and tied the series one game apiece. It was said that: *"James hit a shot that will go down as one of the defining moments in a*

ATOMIC STEPS

career that's just hitting its stride."[15] Tom Withers, AP Sportswriter *May 23, 1:27.*

It is obvious James had practiced this shot repeatedly. Therefore, he believed that he could make it at some point. And he did during that moment of crisis.

Momentum isn't something you reach out and grab. You must be prepared, involved, and inspired. You must work for it. In sports, whenever a team hits a losing streak, they are classified as one that has lost momentum. When they improve their stats, and get back coordinated, they bring momentum back on their side. Yes, momentum takes work to acquire.

I believe in telling stories repeatedly especially if they drive home a particular point. I have told this one on multiple occasions.

I first met this gentleman, a film producer over a decade ago in Los Angeles, California. He had just become one of our tenants in the residential complex that my wife and I managed back in the 90's. He had moved in with his 3-year-old son after going through a difficult divorce. His son bonded with our three boys who were close to his age range. We became friends, and it was customary for my sons and I to hang out with them. visiting on occasion was customary for us. During some of those visits, he asked me to watch his son play, while he caught up on his script reading. This would sometimes last for hours, after which he joined our activities.

ATOMIC STEPS

One of my associates told me that he saw him on an airplane flight with at least six scripts in his bag. Additionally, he read those scripts during the flight. That didn't surprise me because I was accustomed to his work ethic. One year he served as an on-set producer for four movies.

I visited him at his Hollywood office one day before the release of a horror film. There were no big-name actors in the cast. We talked about the film possibilities. He believed that he had a great film. Well, that film has grossed over $100,000,000.00 in box office sales a year. On each of the installments for its run, he has cashed in.

9

VISION

An individual's vision is more often than not tied up in both the eyesight and mindsight. It is said:
Where there is no vision the people perish, Proverbs 29:18 reads. That philosophy and mindset works without fail every time and applies to every area of a person's life. John F. Kennedy the youngest American president said this: "The problems of the world cannot possibly be solved by skeptics or cynics whose horizons are limited by obvious realities. We need men who can dream of things that never were."[1] No

ATOMIC STEPS

Ken Blanchard writes that vision generates tremendous energy, excitement, and passion because people feel they are making a difference. They know what they are doing and why.7 Successful people don't half-step they see it BIG. They see opportunities where failures see a lack of. When a building is being demolished, they see more opportunities in the unconstructed edifice.

I attended an event about a year ago where Robert Kiyosaki was the keynote speaker. Robert, in addition to talking about his rich dad poor dad philosophy based on his book Rich Dad Poor Dad, addressed his prediction of the oncoming recession. Mr. Kiyosaki articulated the importance of accumulating wealth during its tenure and the fact that it would get much worse before it even gets better. The year 2008 has been a tough year for our country economically. It served up a compilation of huge company bailouts, bank mergers, layoffs, unemployment now in the millions, home foreclosures, the closing of several businesses, and the rising cost of health care as well as gasoline.

Any economist will tell you that it's not yet over. They will also tell you that it is the worst it has ever been since the 1929-1939 depression, and the fact remains that we have not yet experienced the bottom of it all. In my opinion, if entrepreneurs and big thinkers don't

ATOMIC STEPS

step up to the plate it could be a long haul for many waiting to score financially.

What are the people with a failure mindset doing? Complaining, becoming cynical. Conversely, the visionaries buckle down and search for ways to create massive wealth. Why? It's a known fact that during a recession most people sell their possessions at huge discounts to survive. The cost of homes has declined drastically and continues to do so. In January of 2009, I was reading a luxury home magazine, which I later loaned to a friend. My friend subsequently picked out a home in Beverly Hills, California, for her vision board. At the time the home was listed at $12.5M.

A month later after church, we decided to take a dream tour of it. The home was now going for $9.5M. I happen to know the seller who is a very successful Hollywood movie producer. He knew that if he didn't sell it quickly, in the next twelve months he could end up selling it for less than half of the initial list price. I returned a month later for a second tour. That house was already in escrow.

Chris Gardener had spent most of his childhood years shuffled between foster homes and other relatives after his mother couldn't adequately support him and his other siblings any longer.

He also struggled to find his way after graduating high school. He later enlisted in the U.S. Navy with hopes of leaving the country. This dream of his never materialized. After several odd jobs, earning sometimes less than $10,000.00 a year, he met a stockbroker who drove a Ferrari plus earned over $80,000.00 a month. Enthused, he decided to become a stockbroker himself and went out persistently knocking on doors of investment firms hoping to find one that would give him a chance. Consequently, he found himself in jail after a police officer ran his license tags and discovered $1,200 of fines in unpaid parking tickets that he owed the city.

After 10 days in jail, he went directly to a job interview with Dean Witter – dirty jeans and all. The interviewer, after hearing his story, sympathized and hired him. Under that bold move on Chris' part, his bio has turned into one of the greatest success stories in American history.

During that interim, he lost his job. His ex-girlfriend left him to raise their 18-month-old child alone. He also got kicked out of his home. While studying for his broker exams, he lived in shelters and a $10-a-night motel with his son. Under his determination, he received his broker's license and was hired by Bear Stearns. In addition, his bio has made it to the big screen. And the rest is history for this man who kept looking forward.

What are your visions for your future? What do you have listed on your dream board? Is it something that wakes you up out of bed excited with the zeal to

ATOMIC STEPS

dominate or do you approach it rather tentatively? Sean, an acquaintance of mine, now in his early 30s, was over $23,000.00 in debt and lived in a garage with his fiancé Loren, without a restroom seven years ago. He got involved in a home-based business. On his dream board, he placed his dream car, a gray Mercedes Benz, a townhouse, and a black and white pen along with other items.

Today, Sean has already earned close to a million dollars in passive income in addition to the gray Mercedes Benz, the townhome that he gutted out and remodeled and that black and white pen that he carries with him all the time. He'd hinted to me about his plan to surprise his bride on their wedding day. Last year I attended their dream wedding. In the middle of the ceremony, he surprised her with the delivery of a gray hard-top convertible BMW. He, an Israeli immigrant to the U.S. now enjoys spending most of his time with Loren while creating a vision for other entrepreneurs.

Humanity, though sometimes anti-visionary, never forgets its dreamers.

Columbus cherished the vision of another world, and he discovered it. Although some didn't help fund his expedition, and many others claimed that he was insane.

Copernicus fostered a vision of a multiplicity of worlds and a wider universe, and he revealed it.

ATOMIC STEPS

Henry Ford visualized, then designed and built his famous Model-T. As a result, today we do not ride around on a horse and buggy.

Dr. Martin Luther King Jr. had a dream that black kids and white kids would hold hands together, and it has happened. To quote Dr. King: "If a man hasn't discovered something that he'll die for, he isn't fit to live."

What visions do you have sitting on the back burner that you genuinely believe can never be accomplished? Dare yourself by bringing them forward! Dust them off! Write them down. You may be keeping accounts, and presently you shall walk out of the door that has for so long seemed to be the barrier of your ideals and shall find yourself before an audience pen still behind your ear, the ink stains on your fingers-and without delay shall pour out the torrent of your inspiration. You may be driving sheep, and you shall wander to the city-bucolic and openmouthed; shall wander into the studio of a great master And after a time the great master shall say, 'I have nothing more to teach you' And now you have become the master, who did so recently dream of great things while driving sheep. You shall lay down the saw and the plane to take on the regeneration of the world." According to Stanton Kirkham Davis.

ATOMIC STEPS

Our world needs men and women with vision, men who are willing to Man up. It also needs women with the tenacity of Rosa Parks.

A vision needs to be strong and unwavering; no one makes it upstream with just a mere wish. If you have a vision and think that you can't accomplish your vision, watch out because somebody else will. Yikes! Tough statement but it's true. Someone else will eat your chocolate-covered ice cream and smile while doing so.

ATOMIC STEPS

The world as we want it to be does not accord with our intuition...those who are successful at creating social epidemics do not just do what they think is right. They deliberately assess their intuitions.

- MALCOLM GLADWELL

10

TIMING

Timing is everything. The famous axiom states: The "T" in timing is better than the "T" in talent. As I mentioned previously if your mom and dad did swing inadvertently you would have ended up in "no man's land." If the sun misses an appointment with planet Earth, we could for a long time be in utter darkness. If the waves miss their timing the ocean will swallow us up.

Timing has much to do with synchronicity but more so with preparedness. Successful people are not only adept at preparation. They rely on their intuition to capitalize on ideas. Therefore, whenever a great opportunity presents itself. They are all over it. Benjamin Disraeli says,

"The secret of success in life is for a man to be ready for his time when it comes,"

ATOMIC STEPS

Abraham Lincoln one of the biggest failures in life said:

"Give me six hours to chop down a tree, and I will spend the first four sharpening the axe."

Let me rephrase in case you missed it, when one is prepared and the right opportunity presents itself, he seizes it and dominates. That's what others call luck. In my opinion, which is Success 101 – the way a high achiever performs.

High achievers love what they do and are at their best doing so. They allow their creativity to operate at the maximum. Conversely, many people allow their creativity to be caged up by doing things they detest doing - simply because it pays the bills. I have seen people with so much potential waste it away behind a cubicle. They would rather be leveraged than leverage others. Many of the successful people I know today welcome business opportunities only if they have leverage. They want to know that they can build something and get paid continually whether they can perform or not. J. Paul Getty certainly understood this concept no wonder. He was the first recorded billionaire.

Today in America "leverage" the word of the wealthy has tremendous sex appeal. With so many layoffs' people are beginning to realize that they need more than having a job. I believe that one of the blessings derived from this recession will be a major

ATOMIC STEPS

entrepreneurial revolution – producing more entrepreneurs than any other economic downturn in our nation's history. My prediction is that the people who make that switch by thinking outside of the cubicle will produce more wealth than many others who have gone before them.

I was recently introduced to Arri, a very ambitious man in his 30s. He made a huge fortune back in his college days in the pager business – way in the millions. At one point, he almost got kicked out of his dorm because of the constant flow of clients. He later sold that business to get into the cell phone business. Very few people owned a cell phone - somewhat of two percent did back then. He was smart enough to place himself in front of that trend. In that business, he made millions and sold it to get into the DSL business when the dial-up was proven to be far too slow for graphics and the much larger files. He has also dominated that industry. Arri thrives on picking the right opportunity at the right time – he positioned himself in front of the trend rather than behind it.

Most successful people aren't lucky; they just master the law of timing. My movie producer friend amassed his fortune through a string of events. After his divorce, he later moved into an apartment complex managed by my ex-wife and me. He made his first big movie, which generated over $35M. It wasn't long before he moved out and bought a house in an upscale neighborhood. When the idea for the horror film was presented to him by a struggling producer who was office-less and sometimes officiated from my friend's office couch.

My friend sold that property, put some money down on another, and used a portion to finance the film. The film has grossed over $100M in its first and subsequent installments. He used his mindsight instead of his eyesight when he purchased that piece of property. His initial investment has now brought him an excess of over $500,000,000, within the last five years. Some said that he was lucky. I don't believe in luck. Real success occurs when preparedness and opportunity meet.

In his bestseller, Rich Dad Poor Dad Investor and businessman Robert Kiyosaki talks about being a professional investor. He claims that the number one key is to find an opportunity that someone else missed. He writes,

"You see with your mind what others missed with their eyes," Kiyosaki explains:

A friend bought this run-down old house. It was spooky to look at. Everyone wondered why he bought it. What that man saw that we did not was that the house came with four extra empty lots. He realized that by going to the title company. After buying the house, the man tore it down and sold the five parcels to a builder for three times what he paid for the entire

ATOMIC STEPS

property. As a result, he made $75,000 for two months of work.5 He further explains: Great opportunities are not seen with your eyes. They are seen with your mind. Most people never get wealthy simply because they are not trained financially to recognize opportunities right in front of them.

As you strive to realize your vision, expect to be criticized and or called lucky. James Allen writes *The thoughtless, the ignorant, and the indolent, seeing the apparent effects of things and not the things themselves, talk of luck, fortune, and chance. Seeing others grow rich, they say, 'How lucky they are!' Observing others become intellectual, they exclaim, 'How highly favored they are!' And noting the saintly character and wide influence of still others, they remark, 'How chance aids them at every turn!' They do not see the trials and failures and struggles that these people have voluntarily encountered to gain their experience; not know the sacrifices they have made, of the undaunted efforts they have put forth, of the faith they have exercised, that they might overcome the insurmountable and realize the vision of their heart. They do not know the darkness and the heartaches; they only understand something clearly at last and joy and call it "luck," They do not see the long and arduous journey but only behold the pleasant goal and call it "good fortune." They do not understand the process but only perceive the result and call it "chance."*

ATOMIC STEPS

Having a vision provides the propellant or the belief to see it come true. However, there's always going to be the naysayer(s) who will tell you that you don't have what it takes to make it a reality. Sometimes, if it is a close friend or relative, they will certainly remind you of those skeletons in your closet. You may excitedly launch your ship but understand that those winds and storms are going to come billowing against you. Trusting their possible caring attitude, you can make that mistake of lending a deaf ear to your unused capacity crying out within you saying,
"You can do it!"

If success was a piece of cake everyone would be successful, then there wouldn't be a reason to go through the cocoon and change. Unsuccessful people remain uncoordinated with success, mainly because they resist change. Ask any winner and they'll tell you that: The major difference between successful people and unsuccessful people is successful people master the art of bouncing back from failure. They keep on keeping on.

Do you know someone who started something but failed to finish it? I know so many would-be authors who begin drafting a book, yet they never finish. It under no circumstances makes its way out of their hard drive. They live a life of "if only I can, or I wish I did." Don't fall into that trap; it's always fully baited with excuses waiting for failures bent on quitting.

ATOMIC STEPS

Launch your dream and pursue it with reckless abandon. Harriet Beecher Stowe declared: "When you get into a tight place and everything goes against you, 'til it seems as though you could not hold on to a minute longer. Never give up then, for that is just the place and time that the tide will turn."

Back in my pre-writing days, I could have said "Let that major movie studio keep their film, do whatever they want to do with it. In Hollywood, it's a rat-race mindset anyway. I wasn't meant to be a writer in the first place. I came here only to act so I'll sit and wait for the auditions. No one wants to read about what I have to say. I'm a high school dropout and on and on... Instead, it was perfectly timed, a blessing in disguise – I heeded that call to write. In the book, The Tipping Point Malcolm Gladwell states: The world as we want it to be-do not accord with our intuition...Those who are successful at creating social epidemics do not just do what they think is right. They deliberately evaluate their intuitions.

If you were to interview the most successful people in the world, they would tell you that one of the keys to their overwhelming success is that they trusted their hunch. Yes, it's like fishing; they felt the nibble and tugged on the line. I believe that when God gives you a vision, he also gives you the ability, and in his timing, you'll certainly reach your destination if you persevere.

11

PURPOSE

In the book, The Purpose Driven Life, Rick Warren writes:

"Living on purpose is the only way to live. Everything else is just existing."

Too many of us drift along with the wrong crowd going nowhere fast. In The Master Key To Riches, author Napoleon Hill recounts a statement by Andrew Carnegie, the man who developed a fortune by going the extra mile:

"The person who is motivated by definiteness of purpose and moves on that purpose with the spiritual forces of his being may challenge those who are indecisive at the post and pass them at the grandstand.

ATOMIC STEPS

It makes no difference whether someone is selling life insurance or digging ditches."

It's a known fact that physically and mentally lazy people tend to remain in their comfort zone for far too long. At that place, no more growth ever occurs. Therefore, they never fully realize the good they often might win by stepping out. Subsequently, the purpose remains unsupported or in most cases undefined. They fail in that effort to grow and stretch. We live in a world full of half-alive people who are no longer sold on themselves. Any professional bodybuilder would tell you that a muscle only grows when it's stretched. The sleeping giants within you need to be awakened. James Allen states in As a Man Thinketh: Those who have no central purpose in life fall easy prey to petty worries, fears, troubles, and self-pitying, all of which are indications of weakness, which lead just as surely as deliberately planned sins (though by a different route) to failure, unhappiness, and loss. For weakness cannot persist in a power-evolving universe. We should conceive of a legitimate purpose in our hearts and set out to accomplish it.4 There's a war to be fought - YOURS! Yes, lifting your head above the crowd will give you purpose, ammunition, and direction in life. You will see where you need to go. And the world always seems to make a way for the person who knows where he or she is going. Streets are crowded; a fire engine is coming through.

ATOMIC STEPS

Everything gives way, pedestrians, vehicles, everything. They all step aside for this speeding machine on a mission. Why? It has a purpose – putting out the fire, and it has a sense of urgency in doing so.

THE CHAMPION

The average runner sprints.

Until the breath in him is gone

But the champion has the iron will.

That makes him "carry on.

For rest, the average runner begs.

When limp his muscles grow.

But the champion runs on leaden legs.

His spirit makes him go.

The average man's complacent

When he does his best to score

ATOMIC STEPS

But the champion does his best.

And then he does a little more.

- Author unknown

A purpose-driven individual will readily discover within that extra-ness necessary to overcoming all odds. The words "I can't" are eliminated from his or her vocabulary. Whenever he's confronted with any sign of defeat he resolves: "I am not giving up, bring it on. It might have licked some but not me. I absolutely will not be denied." Author Julia Cameron writing in her book The Artist's Way says, "I have learned, as a rule of thumb, never to ask whether you can do something. Say, instead, that you are doing it. Then fasten your seat belt. The most remarkable thing follows."

Additionally, she states,

"Take a small step in the direction of a dream and watch the synchronous doors flying open."

A maxim worth remembering, Leap, and the net will appear.

That door one day opened for director Steven Spielberg. He visualized making a unique film. With the script already in possession he needed a producer to finance it. One day while he was walking on the beach, he encountered a man who not only had the resources but was willing to invest in young filmmakers. This total stranger stepped up to the plate and gave Spielberg the money, enabling him to shoot Amblin. That film was given an honorable mention at the Venice Film Festival and opened the door for him to come to Hollywood. The rest is history.

When we know what we want and embark upon accomplishing it, amazing things occur. Let's visit with some purpose-driven individuals who no doubt will take away the excuses of many.

Human Activist, Helen Keller could have said,

"Me? I was born blind and deaf."

Inventor, Thomas A Edison could have said,

"Who needs an incandescent light bulb? I have already tried 10,999 times."

Steve Jobs, the founder of Apple computers, could have said,

"I'm way too young to achieve massive success."

He made his first million at age twenty-three, his first ten million at twenty-four, and at age twenty-five his first 100 million.

President Abraham Lincoln could have said,

"I am a big failure politically. I have already lost eighteen elections. I would never become the American president."

President, Nelson Mandela could have said,

ATOMIC STEPS

"My countrymen threw me in jail, where I've spent most of my life. I could never become the president of my country."

Colonel Sanders, the founder of Kentucky Fried Chicken could have said,

"I dropped out of high school, plus I'm way over 40 - way too old to succeed in life."

He didn't fulfill his dream until age 65 and received 1,009 "NO'S" before he got a "YES."

Paul Getty, the world's first billionaire could have said "I'm not born a businessman. I have no business being in business."

Yet he became a model for some of the most successful businesspeople of our time. Getty said,

"I'd rather have 1 % of the efforts of a hundred men than 100% of my efforts."9 He owns the Getty Museum in Los Angeles, California. One of my associates, about these huge landmark remarks: "Getty owns a mountain and that's the only man I know to do so."

President, John F. Kennedy could have said,

"I am too young to become the American president; no one is going to listen to me."

President, Truman could have said,

"I have not once attended college. I could never become president of America."

Artists, Ray Charles, and Stevie Wonder could have said, "We are blind, how are we going to find the keys to the piano, besides, singing to an audience which we cannot see?"

Charlie Chaplin, one of history's wealthiest actors could have said,

"I grew up in poverty roaming the streets of London. I'll never amass a fortune."

Astronaut, Neil Armstrong could have said,

"The moon is so out of reach I have no business going up there."

Most people lack the initiative needed to become all they were meant to be, mainly because they don't believe, deep down, that they are valuable. Therefore, they live with a purpose-deprived life. Purpose, a directive word, which means heading towards something, gains momentum when meshed with the propellant word belief – that feeling of knowing that you can do whatever you set out to do. People, lacking the propellant in themselves usually look for this additive coming from someone else, and when they don't receive it, they wonder why their life spins around like a tap in mud – going nowhere fast. To take advantage of others believing in you, you must first harness the power of belief in yourself.

When a commercial airplane is getting ready for takeoff, first the doors are closed shut. Passenger's seat belts are securely fastened. The plane then taxis down the runway in preparation for takeoff. The Air Traffic Controllers in the tower see that the plane is ready for

ATOMIC STEPS

takeoff. Instructions are then given to the pilot to speed up. He releases the throttle, retracts the landing gear, and engages the skies.

Believing in you will initiate purpose. Belief: that ability necessary to taxi down the runway in your preparation for takeoff. As soon as others start believing in you, your takeoff becomes eminent. Mark 9:23 states, All things are possible to him who believes. Successful people believed that they were going to be victorious and set sail in pursuit of their objective. Their lives became driven by the desire to succeed. They knew where they were going and consequently, found their hidden guides to take them there.

As an immigrant to the United States several years ago, I sensed that Americans are so fortunate because of the many opportunities, that exist in this country, and that they often take their heritage for granted. Conversely back then I felt like the odds were stacked against me, coming from the Caribbean and not being able to master Standard American English. Nevertheless, I've learned to grasp those opportunities which could lead me to the next level.

Consequently, some amazing people have stepped into my life as guides, including my mentor and friend Bob Wilson. He had just retired after teaching elementary and high school teacher for 35 years. We originally met when he played my Dad in a student film - the adaptation of Guess Who Is Coming To

ATOMIC STEPS

Dinner. This was my initial film project when I moved to Hollywood in 1996. He has always guided me back on the right path, especially during those early years of my divorce, and has played the role of a devil's advocate on multiple occasions. Additionally, Bob has helped me to validate my belief in myself, as I dare to be effective. Bob has an amazing intuitive spirit.

Self-belief is paramount if there is ever going to be any worthwhile accomplishment. Remember, no one else believes in you until you first believe in yourself. If an organization doesn't have a clear purpose and sense of what business it's in, we think there's something wrong. Even so, few people have a clear sense of their life's purpose. How can you make good decisions about how you should use your time if you don't know what business you're in?[1] According to Ken Blanchard in Leading At A Higher Level.

Once you are airborne, then fasten-your-seatbelt signs extinguished, you are now not only committed to flying but at what speed. And most of all you know where you are going.

ATOMIC STEPS

The character cannot be developed with ease and quiet. Only through experience of trial and suffering can the soul be strengthened, vision cleared, ambition inspired, and success achieved.

- HELEN KELLER

12

PASSION

How driven are you towards becoming the success you were meant to be? Some people live their lives in a lukewarm "whatever happens" state. Water is known to boil at 211 degrees and at 212 degrees turn to steam, enough to push any locomotive. That extra degree has propelled many from failure to amazing success.

You, no doubt by now, have developed a sense of purpose. You must. Alternatively, you wouldn't be reading this far. However, do you have a sense of urgency to succeed? Already defined, you know why you exist and your destiny. Even so, permit me to rephrase. Do you have the zeal to make things happen? Without a burning desire, no one will see your

ATOMIC STEPS

readiness. There's enough room at the top but not too many are enthusiastic enough about getting there. That's why they never arrive. They function as if they have forever to live and unfortunately, the successful good life eludes them.

Everything that exists was first an idea acted upon either by you or someone else. As a writer, I have met so many people with ideas for the next bestseller or the upcoming hit movie. Even so, they never write it. Consequently, their idea under no circumstances makes it to the bookshelf or the screen. What would happen if you were told that you only have a month to live? How zealous would you be about getting things done? Would the back burner be empty or still filled with your dreams?

Some people like to watch things happen. Some people like to wonder what will happen, and some people don't care what happens. However, the action-driven person delights in making things happen. Become branded for doing things. When you see something that ought to be done, step up to the plate and hit a home run. Once you acquire the action habit, others have no choice but to step aside for you. Take one step forward in the direction of your goals and dreams, and your enemies will run for cover. They see your value and hear the sirens.

ATOMIC STEPS

In The 5 Steps To Changing Your Life, I also interrelated a story about a young man who was working as a secondhand on a railroad. His thoroughness subsequently won him an opportunity to work in a shipping office.

During the interim, the substitute clerk asked this young buck for some data. The young man didn't know anything about bookkeeping, but he spent three days and three nights without sleep and had the facts ready for the superintendent when he returned.

That enthusiastic act of decision and commitment later propelled him into the vice-presidency seat of his own company. Successful people make it a practice of getting things done while unsuccessful people are routine procrastinators. The successful person sees a great opportunity to go into business for himself while the unproductive person waits until that trend passes him by. He subsequently misses the opportunity to become a profiteer and resorts to the status of a consumer.

Bill, an associate of mine, who made his millions in Network Marketing, recounted to me this story. One day he took several of his top income earners on an island-hopping expedition in the Caribbean. Enchanted by the pretty blue water they took to the seas. Many took that opportunity to show off their water skills. One associate wanted so badly to rank advance and would not let Bill out of his sight. As they

ATOMIC STEPS

swam together, the associate asked my friend: "Bill, I have done everything you told me to do yet I have not advanced. What do I need to do?" Bill remained quiet for a while as he marinated in the question. The water got deeper and deeper.

Finally, he grabbed the associate by his neck, pushed him under, and held him there. The associate kicked and screamed while filling up his lungs with water. Bill released him. He surfaced furious as ever, screaming while spitting out water,

"Bill, what you are doing, trying to kill me? I thought you were my friend."

Bill responded,

"You are my friend. I was only trying to answer your question. See, when you want to advance as much as you wanted to breathe just now - you will succeed."

Life lessons have taught me that great opportunities are captured by those who attack not by those who wait for their ship to come in when they have not even sent it out.

According to William Danforth,

"Each fish that battles upstream is worth ten that loaf in lazy bays."

Danforth also writes,

"Deep down, in the very fiber of your being, you must light an urge that can never be put out. It will catch this side of your life, then that side. It will widen your horizon. It will light up unknown reserves and discover new capacities for living and growing. It will become if you don't look out, a mighty conflagration that will consume your every waking hour. And to its blazing glory, a thousand other lives will come for light, warmth, and power."

IN 1975 BILL GATES DROPPED OUT of Harvard to pursue his career as a software designer. Paul Allen, his colleague, later joined him in the co-founding venture of Microsoft. It was rumored that Gates also showed the concept to two of his other colleagues who said no. Other sources claimed that Gates had a cot in his office that he slept on, night after night for several years when he was getting Microsoft off the ground. In 1980 Gates developed the Microsoft Disk Operating System (MS-DOS). And he successfully sold IBM on this new operating system.

By the 1990s Microsoft had sold more than 100 million copies of MS-DOS making the operating system the all-time leader in software sales.

Gates' competitive drive and fierce desire to win have made him a powerful force in business, but it also consumed much of his life. In the six years between 1978 and 1984, he took a total of only a two-week vacation. Even so, on New Year's Day 1994, Gates married Melinda French, a Microsoft manager, on the Hawaiian island of Lanai. His fortune at the time of his marriage was estimated at very close to seven billion

ATOMIC STEPS

dollars. By 1997 his net worth was estimated at approximately $37 billion, earning him the title of "richest man in America. His contributions amaze me, as is often said, "To whom much is given much is expected."

Aside from being the most famous businessman of the late 1990s, Gates also has distinguished himself as a philanthropist. He and his wife Melinda established the Bill & Melinda Gates Foundation, which focuses on helping to improve health care and education for children around the world. The foundation has donated $4 billion since its start in 1996. Recent pledges include $1 billion over twenty years to fund college scholarships for about one thousand minority students; $750 million over five years to help launch the Global Fund for Children's Vaccines; $50 million to help the World Health Organization's efforts to eradicate polio, a crippling disease that usually attacks children; and $3 million to help prevent the spread of acquired immune deficiency syndrome (AIDS; an incurable disease that destroys the body's immune system) among young people in South Africa. In November 1998 Gates and his wife also gave the largest single gift to a U.S. public library, when they donated $20 million to the Seattle Public Library. Another of Gates's charitable donations was $20 million given to the Massachusetts Institute of Technology to build a new home for its Laboratory for Computer Science.
In July 2000, the foundation gave John Hopkins University a five-year, $20 million grant to study whether or not

ATOMIC STEPS

inexpensive vitamin and mineral pills can help save lives in poor countries. On November 13, 2000, Harvard University's School of Public Health announced it had received $25 million from the foundation to study AIDS prevention in Nigeria. The grant was the largest single private grant in the school's history. It was announced on February 1, 2001, that the foundation would donate $20 million to speed up the global eradication (to completely erase) of the disease commonly known as elephantiasis, a disease that causes disfigurement. In 2002 Gates, along with rock singer Bono, announced plans for DATA Agenda, a $24 billion fund (partially supported by the Bill and Melinda Gates Foundation) that seeks to improve health care in Africa.

Although Gates' parents had a law career in mind for their son, he developed his early interest in computers, which turned into his passion, resulting in the Microsoft phenomenon. His philanthropic lifestyle continues to have an influence.

One December evening in 1955, a seamstress for a department store in Montgomery, Alabama boarded a city bus in route to her home.

It was during the civil rights revolution when blacks were exclusively permitted to sit at the back of a bus. She walked past the "whites only" section towards the middle of the bus.

With frequent stops, the bus filled up. The driver, a white man, noticed that more people of his race were

ATOMIC STEPS

still boarding. So, he ordered the people in the seamstress Rosa Parks' row to move to the back of the bus. They gave him a deaf ear. Frustrated, he barked at those black passengers. They all got up except for Rosa Parks.

Subsequently, this revolting against, enthusiastic act, by Rosa Parks, fueled the already simmering civil rights movement with Martin Luther King at the helm. Consequently, she was arrested and sent to jail after a sheriff was called to the scene.

Today in America, not only are blacks and other minorities permitted to vote but a black man now sits in the White House as our commander and chief. Which situation could you change for the better if you dared to cause a change in the world?

In 2002 I made several phone calls for at least three weeks to find out who held the rights to a 1970s classic film that I so desperately wanted to remake. When I found the studio that did, a woman answered the phone. I told her that I would like to acquire the rights for the film. Her response was "Sorry. We don't give up those rights to any third party." That ticked me off as I was so bent on remaking that movie.

Without hesitation, I called a writer friend who had his script already optioned with a major studio and asked if he'd be willing to help me write my pet project. See, after being denied those rights, I decided that I was going to write my own, and someday they'll come begging for it. My friend told me that because he was signed with a manager it would be impossible for him to collaborate on writing a script with me. Anyway, he sent me templates for writing a screenplay.

I didn't know how to use a computer's keyboard accurately; I had never taken a typing class. Nonetheless, I embarked upon writing my script using my right hand calculating the use of each key while looking forward to seeing what was written on the screen. I wanted to write and did.

Later I showed one of my screenplays to a director I knew. He responded with an email stating that it was the worst screenplay he'd ever read and that I should give it up. As if that wasn't enough, he stated that I was a novice. I didn't write anything for over a week but subsequently returned to the drawing board and wrote explosively. About a year afterward I purposely sent him one of my scripts. A few days later my phone rang. It was him.

"John, how are you, mate?"

"AWESOME!"

I replied.

"Great work! Not too many people know how to write action thrillers. It's a tough genre. You have the knack."

"Thanks,"

I replied even more enthusiastically.

With a few screenplays written and more in the works, including my upcoming Hollywood Story, plus many

ATOMIC STEPS

books already published within the past two years, four of those in less than a year. I'm very excited about what lies ahead. In the words of Helen Keller, Character cannot be developed in ease and quiet. Only through experience of trial and suffering can the soul be strengthened, vision cleared, ambition inspired, and success achieved.

My typing style has not changed much since my writing debut. Even so, I refused to let that temporary handicap fence me in with my vision sitting on the launching pad. I have decided to become unstoppable. I believe in a source greater than me and know that if the thought occurs, it can be written.

13

PERSONALITY

Successful people always seem to exude that indescribable quality that attracts you to them like freckles of steel to a magnet. You feel it in their handshake, their pat on the back. You hear it in their intonations. They're looking you in the eye, and their charismatic smile. They have "IT" and it's called personality. They draw you in. Indescribable, yet it moves you.

Where does personality come from? Is it something with which we are born? Can it be developed? How do we get it? It can be acquired if you are willing to work on yourself.

ATOMIC STEPS

Benjamin Franklin began as a printer's apprentice and later became the first self-made millionaire in America. He adapted a process of personal development. As a young man, he struggled to realize that he was somewhat well-mannered and argumentative, character traits which he realized were creating animosity toward him from his co-workers and associates as well. To change, he rewrote the script of his personality. Franklin began by making a list of what that ideal person should possess. He then concentrated on developing one virtue each week. Some of those thirteen virtues included: tranquility, moderation, resolution, humility, order, and temperance. He practiced and worked hard at these virtues. As a routine, he would practice one virtue each week, then two weeks, then three weeks, and then for one month until it became a part of his character.

As a result, he not only became one of the most popular personalities but also very influential as well. His influence played a very important role as an ambassador from the United States during the Constitutional Convention, when the Constitution and the Bill of Rights for the United States were debated, negotiated, and agreed upon.[5] By daring to work on himself, he made himself into a person capable of shaping the course of history.

ATOMIC STEPS

Some people have a greater capacity for character traits than others. And this has a lot to do with their social upbringing. A child who is raised in a home where love reigns, where both parents' love for each other grows daily, exercises a deeper sense of love for others. That child, because he or she is continuously reminded of being special, being loved, and filled with potential, weighs in higher on the personality quotient. Conversely, the child who grows up in a home where love is lacking on the part of their parents, the kid who is regularly told that they are deficient in so many ways. If adolescents are not schooled in this area, they tend to come in lower on the personality quotient.

The people who've learned from their failures like Benjamin Franklin have been knocked down so many times that they not only embrace "getting back up" with a smile but embrace the adversity simultaneously, knowing that they will get back up, and you better watch out when they do. Successful people tend to turn "IT" on like magic. Their magnetism wins you over in a heartbeat.

I've always made it a habit to learn something from the personality of every successful person I've encountered. Most of all I've noticed and admired this special trait, which is a characteristic of great leadership - the ability to solve problems. Obstacles

ATOMIC STEPS

have no chance, at least not for long. They have that leader's mindset.

Have you ever seen someone enter a room and immediately – charismatically – attract the warmth and attention of others? Understand, they were not born this way. One thing is for certain. They have become this way through their many failures along the way. They have learned how to laugh at and amid their adversities. Personalities who have made success their vocation, are like that whether you meet them on the top of a mountain or down in a valley. In good times or bad, they have a knack for attracting people.

These twelve traits speak volumes about an individual with an attractive personality.

1. He has conquered selfishness. Others have become his priority.

2. He knows that he'll reap what he plants. Therefore, his best gets sown.

3. He exercises self-control.

4. He listens to others.

5. He gives with no strings attached.

6. He recognizes the value in others.

ATOMIC STEPS

7. He appreciates what others intend, not only what they do.

8. He lifts others.

9. He's positive about life.

10. He leads and inspires others. When people leave his presence, they feel better about themselves.

11. He is a servant leader.

12. He keeps increasing his value.

His leadership has influence. He lifts you to higher ground. Brian Tracy, in his book Million Dollar Habits, writes: Make it a habit to go through life doing and saying the things that raise the self-esteem of others and make them feel valuable.

In his book Becoming a Person of Influence John Maxwell writes:

When people feel good about you and themselves during the times, they're with you, then your level of influence increases significantly. You now have a fresh outlook on life with a new feeling about yourself. And because it is easier for you to meet the

ATOMIC STEPS

needs of others once your needs have been met. You become a people magnet. Consequently, a domino effect is created causing others to win because you've won.

14

THE MINDSET

The Free Dictionary defines mindset as A fixed mental attitude or disposition that predetermines a person's responses to and interpretations of situations. Secondly: An inclination or a habit. I like the simplicity of the latter and will refer to it in this chapter. It is said that,
"It takes 21 days to make or break a habit."
All you must do is work at it. If you are afraid of working towards the championship, the sidelines inevitably have a spot reserved for those who are content with letting things happen instead of making things happen.

ATOMIC STEPS

A champion's mindset is never to tiptoe through the tulips in life. Just like a fire engine coming through the neighborhood, they have passion and purpose to fulfill a mission. Dare anyone get in their way!

Let's rewind before proceeding. A champion is prepared, he has conducted a series of learned actions, he believes in his ability, and he has acquired momentum; now he's poised to dominate. In his imagination, the game's over and for him, it's a win. Therefore, he's prepared to lay it all on the line. That discipline, which he brought into his preparation, is now apparent in his game. His work ethic produced confidence and belief in himself - giving momentum to produce a victory.

It has been discovered that the people who lose continually simply don't have the right inclination or habit. If somewhere along the way they have been brainwashed by thoughts of nothingness, they only bring that mindset into the game. It therefore serves as a deterrent and not a propellant. With such a losing mindset, their opponent is going to send them packing.

Boxer Mike Tyson was riddled with controversy surrounding his wife Robin Givens when he entered the ring versus Michael Spinks on June 27, 1988. Before spectators could sit comfortably in their seats, he had already knocked out Spinks at the 1:31

ATOMIC STEPS

minute mark in the first round. We pick up at this part of the fight according to Sports Illustrated:

As the challenger, the 31-year-old Spinks entered the ring first after the long delay. When he removed his robe, his 6'2" body looked trim carrying 212 pounds, his heaviest weight ever, but it was dry. Spinks is a notoriously slow starter; it did not bode well that he hadn't warmed up properly.

By contrast, the 21-year-old Tyson was glistening as he prowled the ring during the introductions, and at the opening bell, he pounced and threw a left hook that caught Spinks high on his head. "I noticed the fear come into his eyes then," Tyson said later. Spinks seemed to sag after the punch, a telling bit of body language common to Tyson's opponents the first time they absorb a solid blow from him. At that moment of violent impact, survival suddenly becomes much more important than victory.

Before the fight, Futch had warned Spinks not to clinch. "We're not matching strength for strength," Futch had said. "That's his game." But Spinks seemed more interested in trying to wrap Tyson in his arms than in escaping harm with a practiced retreat. In their first clinch, referee Frank Capuccino moved in when he spotted the laces of one of Tyson's gloves resting heavily against Spinks' throat.

"All right, stop punching," ordered Capuccino, at which point Tyson's elbow snapped up and his forearm cracked against Spinks' head.

ATOMIC STEPS

"Hey, Mike, knock it off," Capuccino yelled. "Knock it off."

A moment later, as Spinks tried to back away, Tyson snapped his head back with a left uppercut. Spinks was still reacting from that when a short, twisting right hook caught him just below the heart. He dropped to one knee, the first knockdown of his professional career. Spinks was up at four as Capuccino counted to the mandatory eight. "You O.K.?" Capuccino asked, staring into Spinks' eyes.

Spinks peered down at Capuccino. "I'm all right," he said. When Tyson renewed his attack, Spinks tried to fend him off with a right, but it was too soft and moved too slowly. Tyson fired a left hook, shoulder high, over the uncertain right hand. The momentum of Spinks' own punch carried his head forward and down, and Tyson met it with a sweeping right hand. The punch traveled on a waist-high arc and caught Spinks at its most powerful point flush against his jaw. No man could have withstood it.

Spinks' eyes rolled up; his legs quivered. Then he fell straight back, arms outstretched. When Capuccino began to count, Spinks tried to force himself to his feet, but as he began to rise he crashed over on his right side. His head was resting against the bottom rope when Capuccino reached 10.

For Tyson, his brief fight with Spinks — the 35th win of his undefeated pro career — may have been his most peaceful

ATOMIC STEPS

moment in weeks. As the battle for control of his growing fortune escalated, Tyson proved that he comes to fight, and there seems little that anyone can do to distract him.

I'll paraphrase: *As Lewis (Spinks promoter) left the locker room before the fight, Tyson turned to his trainer, Kevin Rooney. "You know," he said softly of Spinks, "I'm gonna hurt this guy."*

And Mike Tyson did, knocking out Michael Spinks at 1:31 of Round 1.

It was all his mindset to win no matter what else was going on. He was totally committed, and nothing was going to stop him. Encapsulating this trait, a champion's mindset is always: "I can! I will! I shall **not** be denied! Whatever I set my heart and mind to do. I will accomplish it."

CASSIUS CLAY, another boxing champion. He later changed his name to Mohamed Ali in 1963. He dominated the boxing ring for almost two decade during the early sixties and late seventies. His mantra echoed, "I move like a butterfly and sting like a bee." Let's pick up from Sports Illustrated, the journey of Ali:

Ali started his boxing career at the young age of 12. He took his first boxing training from Fred Stoner, who was a boxing trainer in Kentucky. His passion and dedication for boxing had placed him in the category of professional boxers, which was a dream for many young amateur

ATOMIC STEPS

boxers of that time. Cassius registered consecutive wins for about six years in the Kentucky Golden Gloves Championship. He also won two 'Amateur Athletic Union Championship titles and two 'National Golden Gloves Championship boxing titles during that period.

Muhammad Ali's career as a boxer elucidates his emphatic wins over some of the great heavyweight kings Sonny Liston, Floyd Patterson, Ernie Terrell, Ken Norton, Joe Frazier, Leon Spinks, and many others. Muhammad Ali's fights statistics show that he defeated many European Heavyweight Champions, British and Commonwealth kings, and other undefeated fighters like Sonny Banks and Billy Daniels.

After winning two 'Amateur Athletic Union Championship titles and two 'National Golden Gloves Championship boxing titles, he set his target for the light-heavyweight boxing category matches. In 1960, he comfortably defeated Zbigniew Pietrzykowski of Poland to claim a gold medal in the light-heavyweight boxing championship at the Summer Olympics in Rome. In 1964, he defeated Sonny Liston and won the World Heavyweight championship for the first time. He defended his title nine times from 1965 to 1967 and became universally recognized as world heavyweight champion. Muhammad Ali's training under Angelo Dundee made him acquainted him with new boxing tactics and styles and helped him improve on some key areas to knock out his opponents.

ATOMIC STEPS

After he refused to be a part of the United States Army during the Vietnam War, he was stripped of his title. Muhammad Ali's boxing career came to a pause, and he was kept away from the fighting ring for the next three and a half years. In 1970, Ali managed to get his boxing license reinstated. Ali regained his title in 1974, when he knocked out George Foreman. He defended his championship ten more times between 1974 and 1978. He lost to Leon in 1978. However, seven months later he again defeated Spinks to regain his title. Ali retired from boxing in 1981. Muhammad Ali's boxing record shows 56 wins and 5 losses. In 1996, Ali was chosen to light the Olympic Flame during the Opening Ceremony of the Atlanta Olympics. Ali was honored with the United Nations Messenger of Peace award in 1998. In 1999, he was also awarded "Sportsman of the Century" by Sports Illustrated.

THE CHAMPION

The average runner sprints.
Until the breath in him is gone
But the champion has the iron will.
That makes him "carry on.

For rest, the average runner begs.
When limp his muscles grow
But the champion runs on leaden legs.

ATOMIC STEPS

His spirit makes him go.

The average man's complacent
When he does his best to score
But the champion does his best.
And then he does a little more.

- Author unknown

Whenever I think of going the distance, my mind races back to this classic story which demonstrates absolute faith. Let's pick it up in Genesis **22:1-12** Sometime later God assessed Abraham. He said to him,
"Abraham!"
"Here I am,"
he replied.
Then God said, "Take your son, your only son, Isaac, whom you love, and go to the region of Moriah. Sacrifice him there as a burnt offering on one of the mountains I will tell you about."
Early the next morning Abraham got up and saddled his donkey. He took with him two of his servants and his son Isaac. When he had cut enough wood for the burnt offering, he set out for the place God had told him about. On the third day, Abraham looked

ATOMIC STEPS

up and saw the place in the distance. He said to his servants,
"Stay here with the donkey while I and the boy go over there. We will worship and then we will come back to you."
Abraham took the wood for the burnt offering and placed it on his son Isaac, and he carried the fire and the knife. As the two of them went on together, Isaac spoke up and said to his father Abraham,
"Father?"
"Yes, my son?"
Abraham replied.
"The fire and wood are here," Isaac said, "but where is the lamb for the burnt offering?"
Abraham answered,
"God himself will provide the lamb for the burnt offering, my son." And the two of them went on together. When they reached the place God had told him about, Abraham built an altar there and arranged the wood on it. He bound his son Isaac and laid him on the altar, on top of the wood. Then he reached out his hand and took the knife to slay his son. But the angel of the LORD called out to him from heaven, "Abraham! Abraham!"
"Here I am,"
he replied.
"Do not lay a hand on the boy," he said. "Do not do anything to him. Now I know that you fear God

ATOMIC STEPS

because you have not withheld from me your son, your only son."

Some may question: Why then would God give this command? As the life story of Abraham later unfolded. It shows that God had major plans and blessings in store for Abraham. And he wanted Abraham to demonstrate his complete trust, placing him primarily, even his son. "His faith was made complete by what he did" (James 2:21-23).

Abraham, therefore, showed that he was worthy of being blessed by the hands of God - He who has everything including the existence of Abraham's son, Isaac.

The Bible is full of champions. It makes me think about how great of a "champion maker" God is.

I RECALL ANOTHER CLASSIC STORY about a special woman in the Bible:

"But Ruth said: "Entreat me not to leave you, *Or to* turn back from following after you; For wherever you go, I will go; And wherever you lodge, I will lodge; Your people *shall be* my people, And your God, my God.

Where you die, I will die, And there will I be buried. The LORD do so to me, and more also If *anything but* death parts you and me."(Ruth 1:16-17 NKJV)

Ruth, a Moabite woman, and daughter-in-law of the widowed Naomi became widowed. Naomi, along

ATOMIC STEPS

with her two daughters-in-law Oprah and Ruth traveled to Judah: the home of the two women.

Expressing her gratitude, Naomi encouraged them to stay behind but they resented; preferring to travel on with her. Naomi pleaded with them, reminding them that she was old and had no plans of getting remarried, and even if she did and had two sons, they would be too young to marry any of the two women. The women wept and Oprah decided to leave but Ruth clung to Naomi refusing to return with her sister-in-law. Ruth had developed a bond with Naomi that was inseparable.

Habitually, Ruth created a mindset that for your love,

"I will never leave or forsake you."

ANOTHER CLASSIC STORY on a commitment intrigues me.

She was referred to as "Moses" not only by the hundreds of slaves she helped to freedom but also by the thousands of others she inspired. Because of her commitment to a cause, Harriet Tubman became the most famous leader of the Underground Railroad to aid slaves, escaping the Free states or Canada.

Born into slavery in Maryland, she escaped her chains in 1849 to safety in Pennsylvania. A feat accomplished through the Underground Railroad,

ATOMIC STEPS

an elaborate and secret series of houses, tunnels, and roads set up by abolitionists and former slaves. "When I found I had crossed the [Mason-Dixon] line, I looked at my hands to see if I were the same person," Tubman later wrote. ". . . the sun came like gold through the tree and over the field and I felt like I was in heaven."

She would spend the rest of her life helping other slaves escape to freedom.

After her escape, she worked as a maid in Philadelphia and joined the large and active abolitionist group in the city. In 1850, after Congress passed the Fugitive Slave Act, making it illegal to help a runaway slave, Tubman decided to join the Underground Railroad.

Her first expedition took place in 1851 when she managed to thread her way through the backwoods to Baltimore and return to the North with her sister and her sister's children. From that time until the onset of the Civil War, she traveled to the South about 18 times and helped close to 300 slaves escape. In 1857, Tubman led her parents to freedom in Auburn, New York, and resided there.

Tubman was never caught and never lost a slave to the Southern militia. As her reputation grew, so did the desire among Southerners to put a stop to her activities. Rewards for her capture once totaled about $40,000, a large sum of money in those days.

ATOMIC STEPS

During the Civil War, Tubman served as a nurse, scout, and sometime spy for the Union army, mainly in South Carolina. She also took part in a military campaign that resulted in the rescue of 756 slaves and destroyed millions of dollars' worth of enemy property.

After the war, Tubman returned to Auburn and continued her involvement in social issues, including the women's rights movement. In 1908, she established a home in Auburn for elderly and indigent blacks that later became known as the Harriet Tubman Home. She died on March 10, 1913, at approximately age 93.

Tubman's eager commitment to love for her people kept her going back until every slave was freed, regardless of the dangers involved.

Whatever your mindset, let it be one of winning against all odds. Only then will you find true fulfillment.

Now, you know what it takes to acquire the champion's mindset. Now you will learn about some of the qualities that define a champion.

15

TEAM SPORT

The famous axiom screams "There's no I in the team." Yet so many people miss it. Champions on the other hand feel the need to be part of a team and embrace this concept. While the "would-be champs" focus on themselves instead of the *whole* and consequently, the championship eludes them. They lose and go home while the other team wins and goes to Disneyland.

The lighted match and the coal must unite if they are ever going to create some heat. Without unity, there could be no production. Could you imagine the coal staying in one corner, chilling out, while the lit

ATOMIC STEPS

match stays in the other spot? Looking across at each other, they yell across the room, "Let's create some heat! Or at least a blazing fire!" and never move into each other's space. It's futile. That match is going to burn itself out and the coal is going to remain unlit and of no importance to each other.

So many "would-be" collaborators remain ineffective because their mindset is trying to do the job alone. They fail to grasp the concept that **T**ogether **E**veryone **A**ccomplishes **M**ore.

No man is an island, and we thrive best when we are working to get her, whatever "her" means for you, the bottom line is "to get." The following story is very much on par with working alone. Let's pick up this accident report.

Dear Sirs,

I am writing in response to your request for additional information. In block #3 of the accident report form, I put, "Trying to do the job alone" as the cause of my accident. You said in your letter that I should explain more fully. I trust the following details will be sufficient.

I am a Bricklayer by trade. On the day of the accident, I was working alone on the roof of a new six-story building. When I completed my work, I discovered that I had about 500 lbs. of brick left over.

ATOMIC STEPS

Rather than carry the bricks down by hand, I decided to lower them in a barrel by using a pulley that was fortunately attached to the side of the building on the sixth floor.

Securing the rope at ground level, I went up to the roof, swung the barrel out, and loaded the bricks into it. Then I went back to the ground and untied the rope, holding it tightly to ensure a slow descent of the 500 lbs. of brick (you will note in block #2 of the accident report form that I weigh 135 lbs.).

Due to my surprise at being jerked off the ground so suddenly, I lost my presence of mind and forgot to let go of the rope. I proceeded at a rapid rate up the side of the building.

Near the third floor, I met the barrel coming down (This explains the fractured skull and broken collarbone). Slowed only slightly, I continued my rapid ascent, not stopping until the fingers of my right hand were two knuckles deep in the pulley — fortunately by this time I had regained my presence of mind and was able to hold tightly to the rope despite my pain. At approximately the same time, however, the barrel of bricks hit the ground, and the bottom fell out of the barrel. Devoid of the weight of bricks, the barrel now weighed approximately 50 lbs. Again, I refer to my weight in block #2.

As you might imagine, I began a rather rapid descent down the side of the building. Near the third floor, I again met the barrel coming up (this accounts for my 2 fractured ankles and the lacerations on my legs and lower body). The encounter with the barrel slowed me enough to lessen my injuries when I fell on the pile of bricks. Fortunately, only 3 vertebras were cracked.

I am sorry to report, however, as I lay there on the bricks, in pain, unable to stand and watching the empty barrel six stories above me, I again lost my presence of mind and let go of the rope, so it came back down and broke both my legs.

I hope I have furnished the information you required as to how the accident occurred. It was because I WAS TRYING TO DO THE JOB ALONE!

In every arena, there's a need for great teams. More men and women would become champions if they were totally committed to playing the team.

In the relationships arena: Some fall in love and expect that the relationship would last if they neglected functioning as a team. Not getting involved would serve both parties better than not being coordinated, so they can pull off a victory.

It's common to hear kids talk about me, me, me, and myself. While the selfish say

"This is my show."

But collaborators say,

"We're in this together. What can we do together?"

16

BURNING YOUR SHIPS

We have now come to one of the most important chapters in this book. This embodies the defining quality between people who succeed and the ones who don't. You know yourself. You have a purpose. You have developed a passion. You acquired a magnetic personality. You created a vision for your life and found the right time to launch it. You leave no road for retreat. In other words, "you burn the ships" the bridge gets demolished. In Think and Grow Rich, Napoleon Hill recounts this story: A great warrior faced a situation that made it necessary for him to

ATOMIC STEPS

decide, which ensured him success on the battlefield. This leader was about to send his armies against a powerful foe. Whose men fearfully outnumbered his. He got busy and loaded his soldiers in boats, sailed to the enemy's country, and unloaded soldiers and equipment. Then he gave the orders to burn the ships that had carried them. Addressing his men before the first battle, he said "You see the boats going up in smoke. That means that we cannot leave these shores alive unless we win! We now have no choice-we win-or we perish!" They won.

All successful people have in common this particular trait. They have learned how to develop the habit of perseverance towards setting and reaching their goals. Their "not giving up mindset and philosophy" separates them from the rest of the world. They know that without determination they will never arrive at their destination. So, they persist despite the obstacles that were presented along the way.

In getting there, they certainly develop patience. That strong character trait is necessary for dealing with all the falls they're about to take. They become masters of the art of getting back up when they get knocked down.

To succeed in today's world and cause a change one needs to not only learn from their failures but also from their successes. They ought to be able to look

ATOMIC STEPS

back at those opposed experiences and say: "This is what I did to succeed, and this is what I've learned. This is what I did that caused me to fail and this is what I've learned from that."

Determination has a lot to do with robust faith. And faith is described as "the evidence of things not seen." It calls for a concentrated unwavering faith, one capable of removing mountains along the way. I moved to Hollywood, California in July 1996 as an actor. Within those first two years, I landed 9 TV commercials in thirteen months.

However, I then experienced a journey dominated by failures. So copious that, constantly being beaten up by life in Hollywood led me to believe every seed I planted was killed by haters and industry pythons alike before they grew up much less bear fruit. Those playhaters who delighted in nothing more than to see my dreams remain on the launching pad. The multiple dream killers who find delight in squeezing my dreams out of me. They had it coming. I decided that I was going to start believing in myself.

I knew where I came from and where I wanted to go. The boy from the islands of St. Vincent and the Grenadines went to school at times without shoes on his feet. I had had enough and was going from here on to make a significant difference. What I touched had to turn to gold. Dare the ones who tried to stop me or get in the way. I was like a rhino coming through. Failure wasn't going to be an option. I was going through whatever stood in my way, in route to my destiny.

I had written several screenplays as I mentioned before but had always wanted to etch my first book. I had unique stories to share. So, on January 21st, 2007, after having a heart-to-heart, a mind over-matter interlude with my hidden guide and mentor the late Dr. Martin Luther King Jr. I took that tremendous leap of faith. I looked at his picture several times, reflecting on what he stood for. If only I could do 20 % of what he stood for I'd be very happy. Releasing just one percent of my untapped potential could make a significant difference in the world.

While pondering my legacy, I knew that I had not done enough for mankind and myself. I stared at MLK's quote: "Take the first step in faith. You don't have to see the whole staircase. Just take the first step."[3] For well over 30 minutes. Consumed by it and all that he stood for, I passionately outlined my first book, The 5 Steps to Changing Your Life.

My contribution towards changing mindsets at this point took center stage. If I could help to change the mindset and philosophy of one dream-deprived individual, this world would become a better place. I reasoned.

ATOMIC STEPS

So, through inspiration, I was moved to write my debut book. That night I opened my writing software, outlined the initial draft, and began authoring that book. I felt as if a dam of inspiration was released from my mind. I kept going back and forth to my book library looking for quotes to supplement my written thoughts. There, I retrieved books that I had previously read. I scanned through their pages, locating the exact high-lighted quote necessary for inserting into the waiting text. I felt possessed with - the Michael Jordan-like feeling when he dumped 69 points on the Cleveland Cavaliers. Inspiration took over.

Consequently, I passionately completed the first draft of that volume in one week.

An editor and cover designer stepped up to the plate as if summoned by some unknown guide. I must admit that I spoke with several designers over a three-month span who promised to collaborate with me on the project but never did. Finally, the right one showed up. He found exactly the image I was looking for and the book was published in June of 2007. I was ecstatic.

The book was subsequently released and made available on Amazon and at other online stores.

One of my clients, a well-known celebrity who I chauffeured learned about my new book and promised to give me a "blurb" after reading its

ATOMIC STEPS

contents. She requested a copy. The book was delivered as requested. I waited for the blurb but never heard back from her. Nevertheless, my book received endorsements from other sources. Meanwhile, my boss, who was her good friend, pulled the PLUG on me - I was out of a job. This turn of events was because someone couldn't see success for himself. Therefore, he didn't want it for me.

Later my roommate at the time said he didn't need the money but because of my velocity. I had taken so many of his excuses away during our dwelling together. See, while he slept, I wrote. Consequently, after weeks of unemployment, I once more found myself homeless. The forces had again emerged. I was back sleeping in my car - A situation for which I was unprepared.

Back in 2007, while my editor edited my first book, I started writing Keep Love Alive. I later titled the volume Spread Some Love (Relationships 101) to cover the basics of relationships. MLK day the next year (2008) rolled around, and I was once again haunted by my lack of accomplishments in life thus far. Despite my recurring adversity, on MLK day of 2008, I printed out the first completed draft of that book. With all the time management skills, I'd gleaned through the years. Without inspiration, I don't know if I could have pulled that off. Inspiration led me to action once again, and I created

ATOMIC STEPS

my break instead of sitting around looking for it. I felt like I was born to write.

In early April that year founded my own publishing company "Books That Will Enhance Your Life." I published the Amazon Kindle edition of the book. A few weeks later the e-book and paperback versions were published and released thereafter.

Upon receiving the proof of Spread Some Love - Relationships 101. I kissed it several times. A friend was with me at the time and jokingly said, "You kissed yourself" For those of you who have seen the book. You will notice that I've used one of my headshots on the front cover. To him, I replied "Yes." If only he knew how much value I saw in this product. I knew that I had brought something of significance to the world.

A particular bookstore chain refused to stock my book on their shelves. They flat out said,

"We are not going to carry that title because the author published it through a small independent publisher" and additionally "it didn't fit our model." That ticked me off because (a) I founded and owned that publishing company Books That Will Enhance Your Life and (b) I authored the book in addition to owning the rights to it. That didn't sit too well with me, so I went undercover.

ATOMIC STEPS

Their booksellers claimed that it was not modeled for their store. Well, based on my research, I found out that if a store wanted to carry a book it was available from one of the major distributors and was returnable. They could shortlist that book. However, instead, they were saying flat out that they were not going to carry the title, "Why?" I pried further.

By this time, I had refused to take their "no" for an answer. In less than three weeks after doing my research and going on a tirade with them, they stocked my book in several of their California bookstores. That led to more stores following suit on the East Coast. When someone said no, I purposefully pushed for the YES and got it.

Through Word-Of-Mouth marketing my book had already arrived on the shelves not only in California but also on the East Coast as well. So much so that the constant flow of orders from that title alerted their corporate office according to their spokesperson. My sub-publisher contacted me to make sure there had not been any fraud involved.

As far as I knew people were just flat-out ordering copies of the book. My phone line was burning up with inquiries about this new title. Friends were telling other friends about it just like a good movie. WOM marketing had the advantage. The small press acquisition department for that book chain dragged its feet with my title submission for national

ATOMIC STEPS

distribution. In the meantime, I'd already secured my first major book signing event with one of their local stores.

The upcoming book signing was creating such a buzz, so much so that a major entertainment TV station proposed to cover me along with the event. However, they pulled out one day before the event. They claimed that they couldn't get a host interviewer to cover for that weekend. I immediately got on the phone and organized my camera crew. Even a freelance stylist provided her services on my behalf.

The day arrived. I showed up excited and dressed to the nines, after all, it was my first major book signing event. All eyes focused on me. The very inspirational on-camera interview ended, and then it was on to the book signing event. In less than a few hours, all the books they had in stock were sold out, much to the surprise of their management team. Their cash registers were going from Cha Ching – to Cha Ching – to Cha Ching. I watched "Spread Some Love - Relationships 101" exited in shopping bags.

Those results still did not influence the small press into a nationwide - in-store placement of the volume. They produced every worn-out excuse under the sun, including me possibly trying a later resubmission of the title.

ATOMIC STEPS

While they were dealing with indecision in that department surrounding the acquisition of my book, the visionary mindset in me operated at full throttle. I was busy creating the script for a docu-drama based on the book. The volume had heretofore sold thousands of copies without any major publicity within the first four months. It was so far apparent to me that people were hungry relationally. Therefore, no matter how long the current recession lasts. I knew that relationship-minded individuals were still going to be working on their relationships. While beating the odds, I squeezed $50,000.00 out of my pocket and despite non-supporting individuals who initially said that they'd participate but reneged during pre-production, the camera rolled.

My former improvisation acting coach had already said yes to helming the project as his directorial debut. I was also busily conducting the dialog with some proposed members of the cast whose commitments were forthcoming. Some of the cast chickened out later. Even so, I was confident about what I had firsthand.

The first day on the set was very emotional. There were no dry eyes, including the cast and crew alike. True love had hit to the very core, validating that I had a great project. From much adversity had come forth "GOOD."

ATOMIC STEPS

IT COULDN'T BE DONE

Somebody said it couldn't be done,

But he with a chuckle replied.

That "maybe it couldn't," but he would be one.

Who wouldn't say till he'd tried,

So, he buckled right in with the trace of a grin

On his face. If he worried, he'd hide it.

Somebody scoffed: "Oh, you'll never do that.

At least no one has ever done it.

But he took off his coat and he took off his hat,

And the first thing we know he began it.

With a lift of his chin and a bit of a grin,

Without any doubting or quiddity,

He started to sing as he tackled the thing.

That couldn't be done, and he did it.

There are thousands to tell you it cannot be done,

ATOMIC STEPS

There are thousands to prophesy failure.

There are thousands to point out to you one by one.

The dangers that wait to assail you.

But just buckle in with a bit of a grin,

Just take off your coat and go to it.

Just start to sing as you tackle the thing.

That "cannot be done" and you'll do it.

--Unknown

In The 5 Steps To Changing Your Life, I recounted the persistence of one of America's biggest failures. It would have been so easy for this young man to bow his head in shame and give up. He failed in business in 1831, he was defeated for the legislature in '32, he was elected to the legislature in '34, his sweetheart died in '35, he had a nervous breakdown in '36, he was defeated for Speaker in '38, he was defeated for elector in '40, he was defeated for Congress in '43, he was elected to Congress in '48, he was defeated for the Senate in '50, and he was defeated for Vice President in '56 and for the Senate in '58. But in 1860, he was elected President of the United States. His name was Abraham Lincoln.

ATOMIC STEPS

You will inevitably find that most successful people have encountered failure along their path. Some of them experienced failure many times, others hundreds of times, while some ranked as high as in the thousands of times – as in the case of Thomas A. Edison. The most important element in their accomplishment is that they never gave up.

Any successful person will tell you that it takes hard work and strong character to succeed. And this goes for all areas of their lives. Several years ago, after my divorce, I got immersed in the subject of relationships and have authored many books on the subject. I've noticed that many people work hard on their jobs and not on their relationships. As a result, they end up in divorce and wonder why their marriage hasn't worked. Determination starts with knowing that you have what it takes to succeed, and therefore, you are not going to be denied. Are you ready for the climb amidst the turbulence to acquire success? How is your thought process?

If you *think* you are beaten, you are,

If you *think* you dare not, you don't.

If you like to win, but you *think* you can't,

It is almost certain you won't.

ATOMIC STEPS

"If you *think* you'll lose, you are lost,

For out in this world we find,

Success begins with a fellow's will-

It's all in the *state of mind*.

"If you *think* you are outclassed, you are,

You've got to *think* high to rise,

You've got to *be sure of yourself* before

You can never win a prize.

Life's battles don't always go

To the stronger or faster man,

But soon or late the man who wins

Is the man WHO THINKS HE CAN!

- Unknown

Not in your life do people get to experience the other 90% of their potential. They experience the thrill of sweet success without exhausting it.
On the other hand, nobody has ever accomplished anything worthwhile without being assessed and

ATOMIC STEPS

tried. Successful people are winners; they let nothing stand in their way of victory. You can smell their tenacity like expensive cologne because they have a feeling of their worth. They think I can. I will and I shall not be denied.

The power of your purpose depends on the vigor and determination behind it. And your determination is necessary to take that ball into the end zone and score that touchdown.

First, you must believe, really believe that you can become successful before you do. "We do not attract that which we want but that which we are." It must be a mindset. And success is a process that takes patience. We live in a microwave age where everything is instantaneous. Immediately, you want this and right away you want that. Well, there is no such thing as instant success. Success is never like the "Jack and the Beanstalk" scenario. It is the complete opposite.

Sometimes other people don't see what we do while we are in the trenches to acquire our success. Most times they only see the result and mistakenly call it luck.

I am always reminded of the growth of The Chinese Bamboo Tree whenever I think about determination. Success calls for great determination. Ask for any success!

ATOMIC STEPS

Most often success is like that Chinese Bamboo Tree, requiring you to hang in there much longer before seeing the fruits of your labor. Many misunderstand the process and view success as throwing on a Superman outfit – such a temporary ordeal. Don't be mistaken, It goes much deeper than that. No wonder it becomes unnerving for most failures to be in the presence of the fortunate for far too long because that victorious person quickly takes their excuses away. According to Malcolm Gladwell in his book Outliers, "What is the question we always ask about success? We want to know what they 're like –what kind of personalities they have, or how intelligent they are, or what kind of lifestyles they have, or what special talents they might have been born with. And we assume that it is those personal qualities that explain how that individual reached the top." He continues: "In the autobiographies published every year by the billionaire/entrepreneur/rock star/celebrity, the storyline is always the same: our hero is born in modest circumstances and by his grit and talent fights his way to greatness."

I must restate: Michael Phelps made it a habit of working out in the pool for 8 hours a day for several years to accomplish Olympic excellence.

WE ALSO FIND THAT failure contributes greatly to one's success. Michael Jordan, the greatest player to play the game of basketball addressed failing this

ATOMIC STEPS

way, "I've missed more than 9,000 shots in my career, I've lost almost 300 games. Twenty-six times I've been trusted to take the game-winning shot and missed. I've failed over and over and over in my life. And that's why I succeed!"

When we think of Michael Jordan, we remember him as "Air Jordan." Some of his stats: Six-time NBA champion (1991-93, 1996-98); MVP (1988, '91, '92, '96, '98); 10-time All-NBA First Team (1987-93, 1996-98), etc. Memories of his failures aren't foremost on our minds. We just remember his achievements. For most of us, we can still see him with his tongue hanging out as he took the ball to the hoop.

DESPITE BEING TURNED DOWN by 403 banks while he embarked upon the quest of raising money to create Disneyland. Walt Disney succeeded and has now brought illumination and adventure to the lives of many kids and adults.

In grade school, Albert Einstein was a very unimpressive student. So much so that when his dad asked the headmaster what profession his young son should pursue, the headmaster replied,
"It doesn't matter, because he will never be successful in anything."

ATOMIC STEPS

The rest is historic. Einstein became one of the greatest physicists of the 20th century. His persistence developed in him the natural gifts of genius.

The Wright brothers, Orville and Wilbur wanted to construct a machine that flew. People believed that it was impossible. "How do you keep that thing up there? Never, it's impossible!" They questioned. In addition, while the two brothers were busily pursuing their invention, scientific studies were conducted to prove that a body heavier than air could not possibly fly. Because of their success, we now travel in an airplane for over twelve hours in the sky across several continents.

The foregoing people are normal like you and me, though because of their uniqueness, they have acquired their unrivaled brand of success. Commonly, though, they have been driven by an extraordinary determination to achieve their individual goals at all costs. Every opposition brought them closer to a "YES." They are adept at turning setbacks into comebacks. Nothing in the world can take the place of persistence. Talent will not. Nothing is more common than unsuccessful men with talent. Genius will not. Unrewarded genius is almost a proverb. Education will not. The

ATOMIC STEPS

world is full of educated derelicts. Persistence, determination, and hard work make the difference. — Calvin Coolidge.

PERSISTENCE is such a fitting word for determination. This special character trait ought to be embodied in the legacy we pass on to our kids. It's a common trend that kids tend to develop their relationship values from their parents. And those qualities they pass on to future generations.

A new bride was one-day making dinner for her husband. He noticed that she cut off both ends of the ham before putting it in the saucepan. He was taken aback and asked: Why such a move? She responded that her mom always cut off the ends of the ham before cooking it, making it very delicious. One day while he was with her mother, he asked her why she cut off the ends of the ham before cooking it. She said she didn't know, and that she saw her mom doing it that way, and it was delicious. One day while with his wife's grandma, he pried further about this ham cooking process. She said I cut the ends off my ham because it was too big to fit in my small roasting pan. It has nothing to do with the taste and texture. I had to cut the ends out of the ham to get it to fit in my pan!

So, just because someone else did it doesn't mean you should do it too because of tradition. Would you

ATOMIC STEPS

be the one to reconstruct your ancestral values thus creating a lineage of future change.

Ask any successful person and they will tell you that going through those walls towards their destiny took persistence and strong determination to succeed. However, once they broke through, their life like that of the beautiful butterfly going through the cocoon became enhanced.

Yes. You acquire the drive and determination to win at whatever you do, whether it's a business venture, athletics, an award, an event, or a relationship. You equip yourself like no other because the goal is to win no matter what. You have a burning desire. When we think of "burning" we think of flames, hot, producing intense heat. So hot, that you can see the white heat. When we think of "desire," we think of something you've got to have, and you won't retreat until it's a done deal. Now combine the two. Add some flaming white heat to that thing that you must have. Now, how badly do you want to win?

In this chapter I have elected to take determination to another level. Some things may sound repetitious. However, we can all agree that success has much to do with repetition.

A burning desire is not just a mere wish, rather it's an unstoppable, undeniable, all-consuming desire. It

ATOMIC STEPS

possesses you. The vision is so real, you can smell it, touch it, and even taste it. It has become something to fight for, something you'll go through walls for, something to die for. We have all seen star athletes who would rather leave their best on the court or the field to keep themselves at the top of their game. We have also seen people who continue to grow to keep up with their income potential - people who go after what they want with fierce intensity.

In this chapter, I intend to take your winning ways to the next level. From now on, whenever you think of yourself, you see winning as inevitable. We are dealing with the mindset of champions and not that of would-be champions or wimps. Winning calls for intestinal fortitude to succeed massively in today's climate. We are talking about people who will leave it all on the line for what they do or for a cause they believe in and wholeheartedly support. We are talking about fighting against powerful opponents of playoff caliber, fighting against dream stealers, principalities, and forces of evil in every arena. Pardon me if these stairs are a little steep for you to climb. If they are, it indicates that you are not ready for the championship, or this book was not meant for you at this time.

Champions are driven to excel and therefore they possess a burning desire to win. We see this in every combative arena. Champions see it, need it, and got

ATOMIC STEPS

to have it. Plus, they grasp the winning concept. The price they'll pay for winning is of no concern. They will go through a wall of linebackers if necessary.

OUR NEXT CHARACTER clearly understands paying the price, for acquiring the woman of his dreams. This classic story is etched in Genesis 29:1-30:24.

Jacob, after reconciling with his brother Esau over taking his birthright continued his trip eastward. It was about afternoon when he reached the outskirts of Haran. There he found shepherds resting near a well, watching their flocks. He greeted them and asked them about the town and his uncle Laban.

During the interim, Rachel, Laban's daughter, arrived with her father's herds. Jacob inquired why the shepherds did not water their flocks while the sun was up. Jacob was informed that the joint efforts of all the shepherds were necessary to remove the rock that covered the mouth of the well. Jacob walked over to the well and single-handedly rolled the stone from its place and watered the herds of Laban.

Rachel was amongst the others who witnessed this amazing feat demonstrated by Jacob's strength. Her excitement climbed to the next level upon hearing that this outstanding visitor was none other than her cousin, the son of her father's sister. She dashed

ATOMIC STEPS

home to tell her father about Jacob's arrival, and Laban went out to the well to greet Jacob and welcome him into his home.

Laban was satisfied with his nephew's excellent service during that first month, and also aware of the blessing that his nephew's arrival seemed to have brought to his house. He wanted to make sure that he would not lose him too soon. He said to Jacob: "You shall not serve me for nothing because you are my relative. Tell me, what shall be your reward?" Jacob replied that he was willing to serve Laban for seven years for the hand of his younger daughter Rachel. Laban agreed, for he knew that he could hardly find a better son-in-law.

Jacob served his uncle for seven years faithfully, giving up sleep and resting in tender care of his flocks. It was said that "God's blessing was with him."

When the day arrived on which Rachel was to be wedded to him, Laban substituted Leah his older daughter instead. When Jacob discovers that his uncle has tricked him, he demands an explanation., Laban responded: that it was not the custom of the land to marry off the younger daughter before the older one. And further stated that if Jacob wished to get Rachel as his wife, he would have to serve him another seven years. Jacob had a burning desire to marry Rachel, so he agreed to do so, and he served

ATOMIC STEPS

Laban for another seven years. After this, he married Rachel, who gave him a son, Joseph.

Jacob was now ninety-one years of age and still an exile and a servant. So, he entreated Laban to let him depart; but Laban could not bear the thought of losing him, knowing of the divine blessing that rested on everything Jacob touched. Therefore, he promised him part of his flocks as a reward for his services, so that Jacob could make his fortune. Jacob stayed on for an additional six years. However, Laban tried all kinds of tricks and ruses to cheat Jacob out of the payment due to him by their agreement. But God blessed Jacob, and his flocks multiplied rapidly until he became a rich man. Jacob's flocks thrived so well that he became the object of much admiration all over the country, and sheep breeders from everywhere came to deal with Jacob. Thus, his wealth was increased many times, and his household was augmented with many servants and slaves.

Assured of his wives' approval, Jacob prepared everything necessary for the long and difficult journey. He did not reveal his intentions to Laban, knowing that his uncle would not let him go.

Jacob knew what he wanted, and it became his burning desire. Therefore, the commitment of his time and efforts were insignificant, when compared to his dream.

To create a burning hot desire, one needs to have the right mindset. Mentally they must be ready to burn

ATOMIC STEPS

their ships, destroy the bridge, and leave no road for retreat.

When we are no longer in survival mode, it becomes a crisis, win, or perish. The crisis mode seems to be the place where most victories occur. Another way to put it is that we are better in war than we are in peace. Someone once said that "we should create a daily crisis in our lives and that will always keep us on the winning edge."

I have several acquaintances who played in the NFL. Now retired, they look for great business opportunities. This demands that they require a burning desire to make it happen. They want to be involved in something that requires a total commitment, not a half-hearted one.

When a champion wants something, they go after it with all they can muster. "Bring it on," he says. "Lead me through the unknown. There I will discover myself and others. If it has never been done, I'll create it. If it demands training, I'll become coachable. The tougher it becomes the better I like it. If it must be it's up to me. Therefore I'll "Man up." If I go down, it will not happen because I wimped out - If I go down, I'm going down fighting. I possess a "pit bull" mentality because I was born to win!" Champions look for something to latch on to. "Give it to me and watch what I'll do with it," they

ATOMIC STEPS

demand. If you desire a touchdown, they crave the pass and carry that ball securely into the end zone.

17
COMMITTED TO FLY

Whenever a commercial airline is getting ready for takeoff, it undergoes a preparatory sequence of activities. These include Doors to the outside securely closed, and flight attendants checking overhead compartment doors to ensure that they are also closed properly. Attendants check seatbelts to see if they are fastened and that tray tables are in the upright position. In addition, emergency procedures are rehearsed in the event of a crash.

As the aircraft taxis down the runway, the air traffic controllers from the tower direct the aircraft to a parking space in final preparation for takeoff. When the pilot receives permission, the pilot releases the throttle, and the once-parked aircraft comes racing down the runway. Picking up speed, it lifts off to the skies – with its wheels retracting in the process.

ATOMIC STEPS

As that aircraft gains altitude, passengers are instructed to then unfasten their seatbelts. The aircraft has reached the point where it is now committed to fly. To further ensure passengers of this, refreshments are then served. Chances of turning back are not a consideration. From the cockpit, the pilot announces the next port of call as well as the approximate time of arrival and the weather conditions there. As it is with a champion, when his mind is made up – it's time to fly.

Preparedness + Action + Belief = Momentum ®. Now that you are accomplished, pertaining traits of a champion, you should be ready to fly. However, there are three questions that you must answer for yourself. How high and how far do I want to go? Who do I want to take with me? and When do I want to begin?

Let's find out about these brothers who were committed to flying:

Orville and Wilbur Wright grew up in the 1800s - 1900s. These brothers wanted to construct an airplane that flew. People viewed them as doubly insane. No one had ever accomplished such a feat. "That's highly impossible," they reasoned. In bars, restaurants, buses, and even churches – everywhere people gathered, this became a topic of discussion. In addition, while Orville and Wilbur worked on

ATOMIC STEPS

their invention, scientific studies were conducted to prove that a body heavier than air could not possibly fly.

Here's more on their journey:

In 1899, after Wilbur Wright had written a letter of request to the Smithsonian Institution for information about flight experiments, the Wright Brothers designed their first aircraft: a small, biplane glider flown as a kite to assess their solution for controlling the craft by wing warping. Wing warping is a method of arching the wingtips slightly to control the aircraft's rolling motion and balance.

The Wrights spent a great deal of time observing birds in flight. They noticed that birds soared into the wind and that the air flowing over the curved surface of their wings created lift. Birds change the shape of their wings to turn and maneuver. They believed that they could use this technique to obtain roll control by warping or changing the shape of a portion of the wing.

Over the next three years, Wilbur and his brother Orville would design a series of gliders that would be flown in both unmanned (as kites) and piloted flights. They read about the works of Cayley, and Langley, and the hang-gliding flights of Otto Lilienthal. They corresponded with Octave Chanute concerning some of their ideas. They recognized that control of the flying aircraft would be the most crucial and hardest problem to solve.

Following a successful glider test, the Wrights built and evaluated a full-size glider. They selected Kitty Hawk,

ATOMIC STEPS

North Carolina as their test site because of its wind, sand, hilly terrain, and remote location.

In 1900, the Wrights successfully assessed their new 50-pound biplane glider with its 17-foot wingspan and wing-warping mechanism at Kitty Hawk, in both unmanned and piloted flights. It was the first piloted glider. Based on the results, the Wright Brothers planned to refine the controls and landing gear and build a bigger glider.

In 1901, at Kill Devil Hills, North Carolina, the Wright Brothers flew the largest glider ever flown, with a 22-foot wingspan, a weight of nearly 100 pounds, and skids for landing. However, many problems occurred: the wings did not have enough lifting power; the forward elevator was not effective in controlling the pitch; and the wing-warping mechanism occasionally caused the airplane to spin out of control. In their disappointment, they predicted that man would probably not fly in their lifetime.

Despite the problems with their last attempts at flight, the Wrights reviewed their test results and determined that the calculations they had used were not dependable. They decided to build a wind tunnel to assess a variety of wing shapes and their effect on lifts. Based upon these tests, the inventors had a greater understanding of how an airfoil (wing) works and could calculate with greater accuracy how well a particular wing design would fly. They planned to design a new glider with a 32-foot wingspan and a tail to help stabilize it.

ATOMIC STEPS

In 1902, the brothers flew multiple test glides using their new glider. Their studies showed that a movable tail would help balance the craft and the Wright Brothers connected a movable tail to the wing-warping wires to coordinate turns. With successful glides to verify their wind tunnel assesses, the inventors planned to build a powered aircraft.

After months of studying how propellers work the Wright Brothers designed a motor and a new aircraft sturdy enough to accommodate the motor's weight and vibrations. The craft weighed 700 pounds and came to be known as the Flyer.

The brothers built a movable track to help launch the Flyer. This downhill track would help the aircraft gain enough air speed to fly. After two attempts to fly this machine, one of which resulted in a minor crash, Orville Wright took the Flyer for a 12-second, sustained flight on December 17, 1903. This was the first successful, powered, piloted flight in history.

In 1904, the first flight lasting more than five minutes took place on November 9. Wilbur Wright flew the Flyer II.

In 1908, passenger flights took a turn for the worse when the first fatal air crash occurred on September 17. Orville Wright was piloting the plane. Orville Wright survived the crash, but his passenger, Signal Corps Lieutenant Thomas Selfridge, did not. The Wright Brothers had been allowing passengers to fly with them since May 14, 1908.

ATOMIC STEPS

In 1909, the U.S. Government bought its first airplane, a Wright Brothers biplane, on July 30. The airplane sold for $25,000 plus a bonus of $5,000 because it exceeded 40 mph. In 1911, the Wrights' Vin Fiz was the first airplane to cross the United States. The flight took 84 days, stopping 70 times. It crash-landed so many times that little of its original building materials were still on the plane when it arrived in California. The Vin Fiz was named after a grape soda made by the Armour Packing Company.

As a result of their commitment to fly, we can now travel in an airplane from New York to London, Paris, Rome, and other cross-continental cities in less than six hours. Many of us are afraid to launch out. The word commitment scares them, mainly because they are afraid of failing. If you want to become a champion, it is a good thing to jump off with your ideas and see who will catch you. You just never know!

ATOMIC STEPS

18

THE END IN MIND

Champions are very visionary. They look beyond their performance with an end in mind. They see themselves receiving the Oscar, the Grammy, the Nobel Prize, the trophy, the gold medal, the diploma, or the award. They see themselves fulfilling their destiny. Dr. David Bremer writes in the *Spirit of Apollo*, "The world wants your best, and you should resolve early in life never to give anything but the best of which you are capable." The people who achieve massively give nothing but their best to produce a victory.

The words "I can't" are eliminated from their vocabulary. If obstacles are placed in their way, they go around them, go through them, go under them, go over them, or with divine intervention detonate

ATOMIC STEPS

them. Yes, high achievers have and depend on their spiritual connection to remove mountain-like challenges along the way. Most will develop an irremovable faith in God to watch problems disappear. I've seen it happen in the lives of many.

I impart to you this story about my pastor's wife, Holly Wagner. Holly is known for her key role in empowering women around the world, her contribution to social justice, as well as helping a large multi-racial non-denominational church in the heart of Hollywood, California.

A few years ago, Holly was diagnosed with breast cancer. Though our church believes in miracles and the power of prayer, we watched her fight this disease with the power of words. I saw her a few times during her battle and found out that she carried around index cards with words of confession and affirmation; she didn't want anything to do with the sometimes fatal disease.

Prayers were poured out on her behalf, and it's believed that she confessed her healing. Holly possessed a vision of tremendous service to not just Hollywood but around the world. Today, she travels all over the world teaching people the power of the Word over sickness in the body as well as building strong and healthy relationships.

Champions are known to speak what they want in advance. Knowing that like a computer, **input** =

ATOMIC STEPS

output. They know what they sow in speech and thoughts they are going to reap in outcome. Some of their self-talk includes some of the following:

- No weapon formed against you shall prosper. (Isaiah 54:17 NKJV)

- "I can do all things through Christ which strengthened me." (Phil. 4:13 KJV)

- "The steps of a good man are ordered by the Lord." (Ps. 37:23 KJV)

- I refuse to renounce my self-image, no matter what happens to me.

Some of my favorite inspirational one-liners from Bishop T.D. Jakes's messages are:

- The battle is not mine; it belongs to the Lord.

- What God has for me no devil in hell can take.

- I was born to do this.

ATOMIC STEPS

- The time has come for my change.

- God is taking me where no man has gone before.

- I must prosper.

- I can have what God says I can have.

- I will rise! I will finish.

- When it's all said and done, I'll come out of it.

- I'm the head and not the tail.

- You may whip some but not me. I'm going to force you to give up.

- I have what it takes for my dream.

- I'm a giant killer.

- I'm chosen. I can take less and do more with it.

ATOMIC STEPS

- God wants me to be so blessed that I live in the land of much.

- God is opening doors for me that no man can shut.

This story embodied the power of speaking what you want:

MB, a young man in his mid-20s, moved from Northern California to Hollywood over a year ago in pursuit of the Hollywood dream. I met him at our church while he was still getting acclimated, and we created a bond; he has admirable leadership potential. As most people who move to the entertainment industry capital know, you take the job you can get until you get the job you want. So, he took a management position at a retail store, a job that demanded him to show up to work on Sundays. I could tell he was burnt out Sunday after Sunday.

MB told me that he had had enough and was ready to move on. I saw him a week after that conversation, and he mentioned to me that he scheduled an interview with one of the top talent agencies in the industry. He was confident about landing the job. He said,

"I'm going to get it."

ATOMIC STEPS

I was a little hesitant but suggested an alternative agency just in case. He looked me dead in the eye and said,
"John, I'm going to get it."
A few days later my phone rang. It was MB and he had gotten the job. MB said what he wanted and got it. It's almost 3 years since and he's progressing within that agency. His reaping had much to do with his sowing.
To reap bountifully a champion sows. He anticipates the harvest, but he concentrates on his sowing.

AS A CHILD, I LEARNED this invaluable lesson on sowing and reaping:
I'm always reminded of many childhood experiences including watching my parents exercise their farming skills. First, they prepared the land by removing the rough shrubbery and then plowed the land. Then they sowed corn in anticipation of a harvest. After a few days, the little corn plants sprouted. The corn was then watered and fertilized. Weeds shot up attempting to destroy the now-growing green acres of corn. My parents summoned two of my other siblings and me, to embark on not only molding those plants but destroying the treacherous weeds. Like destroyers, we moved in with our hoe (an iron tool used to prepare the land and remove weeds). We whacked those weeds out

ATOMIC STEPS

and laid them to rot next to the corn plants - providing fertilizer for the now aggressively growing corn. It wasn't long before ears of corn were popping up everywhere. The birds came to get fed. We were once again summoned and moved in with sticks which we inserted into the ground and tied black plastic bags to them. These served as a deterring object which as the wind blew chased the birds away.

It was now harvesting time and we picked multiple baskets of corn. My parent's vision was now a reality as those ears of corn were sold at Friday's market. Not only that, but we also cooked, roasted, baked, and ground corn for consumption.

Farmers, like champions, approach life with the mindset and philosophy of an end in mind. Knowing what they sow, they will also reap. Therefore, they are committed to the sowing process. Even if their harvest comes within the time limit of a Chinese Bamboo Tree, they are committed, not for the short term but for the long haul.

I am always amazed by people's mindset as they set their New Year's resolutions. Before that new year, they sit down and methodically plan their entire year. They list all those things about them that they detest and ultimately want to change.

They will go as far as to put a time limit on the changes of those vices. Additionally, they will list

ATOMIC STEPS

their dream for a better year than the one they just lived through.

According to surveys done in 2005, only 8 percent of Americans successfully achieved their New Year's resolutions. A colossal 45 percent fail by the end of January!

When it comes down to total commitment, if you desire heat you have to first put wood in the stove. Let me encapsulate: **Preparedness x Action x Belief x Momentum = A Champion's Mindset®.**

What are you committed to, this year, this month, this week, this day, this hour, this minute? What will commit to during your occupancy on this planet? What can you commit to if you know that failing at it is impossible?

The champions of today dominate in every industry, sport, or endeavor. Why? Because they chose to win! Don't let this book become just another personal development volume in your collection. As you finish these pages, find your WHY – that is something you are willing to commit to.

ATOMIC STEPS

Nothing in the world can take the place of persistence. Talent will not. Nothing in the world is more common than unsuccessful people with talent. Genius will not. Unrewarded genius is almost a proverb. Education will not. The world is full of educated derelicts. Persistence, determination, and hard work make the difference.

— Calvin Coolidge

ATOMIC STEPS

19
CHANGING YOUR CHARACTER

Who are you really when no one is looking? "Man know thyself," the famous axiom urges. Changing your character is the most thought-provoking, and sometimes dreaded, step toward changing your world. If you embrace this change, you are ready to swim upstream where, like a diamond in the rough, you'll become polished and will no longer remain hidden with your light under a bushel. Changing your character calls for that mustard-seed-like faith and self-discipline that will enable you to scale mountains along the way.

YOUR CHARACTER DEFINES YOU

In August 1963 in a speech to civil rights supporters at the March on Washington, Martin Luther King Jr. declared,

ATOMIC STEPS

"I have a dream that my four little children will one day live in a nation where they will not be judged by the color of their skin but by the content of their character."

He wanted his family to be defined by their character.

When I was a little boy, I recall my mom dragged my eight siblings and me to church every week, even if our worship attire had to be recycled. She insisted on our involvement. She was proud of us and the foundation that was being laid in the lives of her kids. That weekly two-mile walk each way not only wore out our shoes but also helped develop fortitude in us.

Immediately after my divorce in 2000, I found myself homeless. As a result of 9/11, TV commercial auditions were very rare, and most of my currently running commercial spots got cut. I watched as my savings accounts plummeted to zero.

My employment search continued after my unemployment benefits expired, but it seemed like the spots of the person with leprosy were tattooed onto my body; no one opted to hire me. So, I prayed. And fasting was automatic and habitual. But most importantly, my trials summoned the faith lessons I had learned as a child. That faith merged with what I was learning, and my search for wisdom

ATOMIC STEPS

skyrocketed. My writing skills improved, too, so I continued writing.

I became a better listener during this time and experienced the Holy Spirit speaking to me often in a still small voice, reminding me that I was chosen. I grew to believe that the world needed me as well as I needed it. My car became not only a place of rest but also an office after Starbucks closed its doors for the night. I wrote every day no matter what, focused on getting back on the horse. My mantra was like a broken record: you kick me when I'm down but watch out when I get back up.

In retrospect, I realize that a tremendous groundwork was laid during my childhood, and I thank and applaud my parents (my mom as well as my dad, who died when I was 9) for what they did. My life has been one of testing, and through the fire, I've emerged stronger than when I went in and appreciative of the refining process.

Will you have to face the challenges I've faced? I hope not. But whatever challenges you might be going through right now, whether financial, health-related, or based on relationships or your career, you can come out of them if you realize that you are chosen and have unquenchable passion and purpose for your life. As Norman Vincent Peale said,

"You can if you think you can."

ATOMIC STEPS

DEVELOPING PASSION AND PURPOSE

"But they that wait upon the Lord shall renew their strength; they shall mount up with wings as eagles; they shall run and not be weary; and they shall walk, and not faint." (Isa. 40:31 KJV)

What do you want said of you when your physical journey has ended? Wouldn't you rather wear out than rust out? Is it your intent to achieve something that will make the future point to you with even more pride than the present is pointing to those who have gone before you? What is your purpose? Is it for a cause greater than yourself?

So many people resist change for fear of the unknown. But if they were to stretch outside of their comfort zone, they would be amazed at the beautiful rainbow waiting to pour down showers of blessing upon them. Most people don't want to stretch, and they go to their graves with music still inside of them.

Their epitaphs read:

"No guts no glory."

If you've gotten this far and are committed to this journey, you have what it takes to finish strong. Life is about obeying *you*. I dare you to get immersed in your life's mission, whatever it may be. There's no half-stepping. When you move tenaciously in the direction of your vision, your vision moves

ATOMIC STEPS

tenaciously toward you. "No man can stop the man with a plan because no one has a plan to stop him" (unknown).

How long will you keep on keeping on? It would have been so easy for one young man to bow his head in shame and give up.

Sir Winston Churchill learned much about perseverance. He said,

"Success is going from failure to failure without loss of enthusiasm."

A few days after he was elected Britain's Prime Minister in 1940, the 65-year-old delivered his famous "blood, toil, tears and sweat" address:

Victory is our aim, victory at all costs, victory despite terror, victory, however long and hard the road may be; for without victory, there is no survival.[5] He also said: *There comes a special moment in everyone's life, a moment for which that person was born. That special opportunity, when he seizes it, will fulfill his mission – a mission for which he is uniquely qualified. In that moment he finds greatness.*

Churchill led with courage and strong determination. "His bull-dog determination smashed through every obstacle that stood in the road of victory. Dubbed the "bulldog warrior," Friend and foe alike knew the meaning of his raised two forefingers which formed a "V" –victory at all costs.[7] When passion blends with purpose, an

ATOMIC STEPS

unbeatable force emerges. Like a tidal wave, it lifts the possessor toward what some would call unattainable heights.

On a Thursday evening in December 1955, after a long day of work as a seamstress for a Montgomery, Alabama, department store, a woman named Rosa Parks boarded a city bus in route to her home.

She walked past the first few mostly empty rows of seats marked "Whites Only." It was against the law for an African American to sit in those seats, so she occupied a seat in the middle of the bus. After several stops, the bus maxed out. The driver noticed that all the seats in the "Whites Only" section were taken and that more white passengers had just boarded. He ordered the people in Mrs. Parks' row to move to the back of the bus, where there were no open seats. At first, no one budged. But then the driver barked at the black passengers a second time and they all got up, except for Rosa Parks.

Subsequently, the Sheriff was called in and Rosa Parks was arrested and sent to jail. Her act of passion led to the eruption of the already simmering Civil Rights Movement with Martin Luther King Jr. at the helm — a movement that has given previously denied rights to blacks and other minorities.

ATOMIC STEPS

GETTING BACK ON OFFENSE

The life of Helen Keller, an inspirational author and activist who was both blind and deaf, takes away the defense of those who use petty excuses for failure to rise in the world. She wrote, "Character cannot be developed in ease and quiet. Only through experience of trial and suffering can the soul be strengthened, vision cleared, ambition inspired, and success achieved."

When I embarked upon my writing career, there was no time to learn the keys on the keyboard; a high school dropout, I had never taken a typing class. But I wanted to write. It was as if a dam of inspiration had burst open. So, my right hand did the talking while the keyboard did the walking. Today, several scripts and a book later, I still type with my right hand. Some people wait for the right moment to do things. For them, everything must be perfect before seizing the opportunity. But great achievers have an abundance of "iron in their blood" and accomplish worthwhile feats, obstacles, or no obstacles. Author Dr. Sidney N. Bremer says in his book *Spirit of Apollo*, "No matter what your position in life may be or the conditions which hem you in, there will be a tide in your affairs which, taken at its flood leads on to fortune. But you must be ready to take that chance."

ATOMIC STEPS

So many people allow handicaps to keep them from achieving victory. A man of character sees a victory in every adversity. There could have been hundreds of people with the potential of Abraham Lincoln, Rosa Parks, Martin Luther King Jr., Winston Churchill, and Helen Keller born during their time. But because those hundreds resisted change, their contribution to mankind remains undefined.

Change is tough because it takes you out of your comfort zone. It stretches you and puts you face-to-face with the unknown. In the Bible, Jacob's real change occurred after he wrestled with God. Once you embrace change, the Creator will provide the supernatural resources necessary to impact your life. He will build a bridge across the gulf of impossibility, but it's up to you to accept the adventure and cross that bridge. There's no more impressive sight in society than that of a young man fired up with passion and purpose. He's bound to win; the world stands aside to let him pass.

DREAM BIGGER

How big is your dream? Is it a cause greater than yourself? You will not make it upstream with only a mere wish. The rapids are fierce; they'll push you back downstream toward self-pity and mediocrity if your resolve isn't strong enough.

ATOMIC STEPS

NINE KEY POINTS TO REALIZING YOUR DREAM

1. Focus on a big dream that includes others; By empowering others you will in turn become empowered.

2. Start with whatever is in your heart right now and trust your hunch — that invisible voice that breathes life into your vision. Someday your acorn of desire may become a full-grown oak.

3. Increase your self-worth by trusting in the power greater than yourself. Put God in the driver's seat.

4. Become enthusiastic about your vision. Aim high, work hard, and think creatively, and the dream that others call impossible will be yours for the taking. They will eventually applaud you as you cross the finish line.

5. Tenaciously pursue your dream in the face of setbacks, even failures. Stay focused. Failure itself is never the tragedy; low aim is the

ATOMIC STEPS

tragedy.

6. Watch out for dream stealers. They come in the form of family and well-meaning friends. Just about anybody will say no to your idea, and you'll have multiple reasons for quitting along the way. It's always the finish — not the start — that counts.

7. Do something daily to nurture and support your dream. Remember, the dream isn't worth having unless you enjoy the journey.

8. Prepare yourself mentally. As Louis Pasteur said, "Chance favors only the prepared mind."

9. Be persistent. A huge tree doesn't tumble with one swing of the axe. You've got to keep swinging. If you can dream it, you can have it.

VISION IS THE KEY

Your aim needs to be as bold as your courage, not as timid as your fear. German poet Johann Wolfgang von Goethe said this:" Whatever you can do, or dream you can do, begin it. Boldness has genius, power, and magic in it." Author James Allen stated,

ATOMIC STEPS

"Columbus cherished a vision of another world, and he discovered it; Copernicus fostered a vision of a multiplicity of worlds and a wider universe, and he revealed it."
Martin Luther King Jr. dreamed of an America where black kids and white kids would hold hands and walk together and it has happened. Humanity, though sometimes anti-visionary, never forgets its dreamers.
The man who has triumphed over difficulty — who has a vision and achieves it — bears signs of victory on his face. He seems to glow with triumph in every movement. The winner's circle embraces him.

DEVELOP A MAGNETIC PERSONALITY

What you love and how you love defines who you are. Have you ever seen someone enter a room and immediately — charismatically — attract the warmth and attention of others? Some personalities are like that. Whether you meet them on top of a mountain or down in a valley. In good times and in bad, they have a way of attracting people.

These twelve things can be said about such a person:

- He has conquered selfishness; others have become his priority.

ATOMIC STEPS

- He knows that he will reap what he sows.

- He exercises self-control.

- He listens to others.

- He gives with no strings attached.

- He recognizes the value in others.

- He appreciates what others intend, not only what they do.

- He lifts others.

- He's positive.

- He leads and inspires others.

- He possesses a servant's heart.

- He keeps increasing his value.

John 3:16 is one of the most profound passages of scripture. It tells us this: "God so loved the world that he gave his one and only Son so that whosoever

ATOMIC STEPS

believeth in him may not be lost but have everlasting life."

This verse represents love unabridged. It shows that God is love. He delights in coming through for you just as He did for the three Hebrew boys in the fiery furnace, Daniel in the lions' den, and the children of Israel crossing the Red Sea. In love, He offers you eternal life through His Son, Jesus Christ.

How do you love others? James 2:8 says, "This royal law is found in the scriptures: 'Love your neighbor as you love yourself.' If you obey this law, you are doing right." Jesus painted this picture in the story of The Good Samaritan, who stepped up when the religious people of his day overlooked a man who was robbed, beaten, and left by the side of the road (Luke 10:25-37).

"From everyone who has been given much, much will be demanded." Luke 12:48 says. There's something special about a child of God who has gone through tough times and gotten back up. Have you ever been in the sphere of such an individual and felt blessed? It's inescapable! That person has developed a strong relationship with God out of a need to seek and find Him regularly. He has created such a bond with God that the overspill has become contagious, setting off a brush fire of love in your heart. You want to be around that kind of person.

ATOMIC STEPS

After a decade-long fight with leukemia, the teenage daughter of one of our pastors and my great friend, went home to be with the Lord. At the memorial service in her honor, I watched as tremendous amounts of love poured out from the congregation, mainly from couples who had been coached by Gary and his wife, and some whom he had joined in holy matrimony.

A few weeks later I had lunch with him. As we broke bread together, verses of scripture poured from him like a flowing stream. I united pen and paper, trying not to miss a thing. Not once did he talk about his loss. But what he had gained was worth my documenting: an abundance of God's rich promises. When we parted that afternoon, I left spiritually filled. He's a man of stalwart character, and I'm proud to call him a friend.

DEVELOP FRIENDSHIPS

When you want to convert a man to your view, you go over to where he's standing, take him by the hand, and guide him; you don't call him a dummy; you don't order him to come over where you are. You start where he is, and work from that position. That's the only way to get him to budge. — Thomas Aquinas

ATOMIC STEPS

To paraphrase Mr. Philip Wagner from his "iLove" message that stirred me:

- Accept people and embrace their differences. Throw out the mindset of "If you pass my battery of tests, then I'll love you." Remember: To love is natural, but to love unconditionally is supernatural.

- Demonstrate acts of kindness. Give legs to the love you have for someone by showing it in practical ways, as God has for us. Remember: People don't care what you know until they know how much you care.

- Make a connection. It's possible to work, hang out, and even live with someone without making a meaningful connection. Connecting requires openness, honesty, and sharing of your life. Remember: People love to talk about themselves.

- Be loyal. Earn the trust of others, and don't take for granted the most trustworthy people in your life. Express love and appreciation for them more than anyone else. Remember: Loyal friends are hard to find and harder to keep.

ATOMIC STEPS

Love should be like a never-ending stream. The more you pour out, the more you find to pour.

LEAD BY EXAMPLE

Leadership is all about character. A true leader inspires followers, and to develop leaders, you must become a better leader yourself. That comes with changing and growing.

In his book *Life is Tremendous,* Charlie Jones states, "Everyone is responsible for something he alone must do. If we enjoy the privilege and discharge our obligation, we grow; if we ignore our opportunity, we join the shrinking violets of humanity. The most tremendous experience of life is the learning process. The saddest time is when a person thinks that he has learned enough."[16] God has given each of us talents and abilities just as he did in the story of the ten talents (Matt. 25:14-30). What we do with what we've been given determines who we are. We either *use* it or *lose* it.

Great leaders use what's been given to them and are not afraid to fail. They're cut from the fabric of persistence. Education is not always a requirement for such a calling, and most begin with genuine handicaps.

ATOMIC STEPS

Nothing in the world can take the place of persistence. Talent will not. Nothing is more common than unsuccessful men with talent. Genius will not. Unrewarded genius is almost a proverb. Education will not. The world is full of educated derelicts. Persistence, determination, and hard work make the difference. — Calvin Coolidge

To lead, you must have someone following you. And to have a following, you must develop trust. Trust lies at the core of strong character formation. "No man can climb out beyond the limitations of his character,"[18] John Morley said. Just as the "things which proceed out of the mouth come from the heart and they defile the man" (Matt. 15:18 KJV), a lack of trustworthiness in a person shows weak character.

BECOME A WINNER

Losers let things happen, but winners make things happen. Winners are never satisfied with who they are, and therefore, they're constantly changing and enhancing their self-image. They have a vision of the person they want to become, and they develop a well-defined, emotional picture of themselves as if they have already achieved that goal. Advance-winning pumps through their veins.

- They breathe the championship.

ATOMIC STEPS

- They feel drenched from the entire bucket of Gatorade poured over their heads.

- They experience the thrill of Disneyland before playing the Super Bowl.

- They caress the Oscar.

- They hear the crowd's approval.

- They feel the gold medal around their neck.

- They see a church with one million members worshipping in spirit and truth.

- They stand tall in the winner's circle.

- They feel their new self-image in advance.

- They dress and rehearse receiving the Nobel Prize.

Winners let nothing stand in the way of victory. You can smell their tenacity like expensive cologne because they have a feeling of their worth. They think, "I can, I will, and I shall not be denied."
The power of your objective depends wholly on the vigor and determination behind it.

ATOMIC STEPS

To paraphrase Dr. Bremer: Your resolute will and firm determination to succeed will carry you upstream, no matter how strong the current or how tough the obstacles in your way. But if your will is fragile and your determination wavering, you will float downstream with the multitudes of others who, like a dead fish, have not enough zest or willpower to force their way upstream.

A reservoir of water will not quench a city's thirst, nor put out fires if it is not allowed to circulate in the mains and service pipes.
— Sidney N. Bremer

ATOMIC STEPS

20

CHANGING THE WORLD

D r. Sidney Bremer, the author of Spirit of Apollo wrote,
"Nothing and no one but yourself can prevent you from attaining your ambition. What one man can do, or has done, reveals an open door that all others may enter. We've not only got to believe, but we've also got to expect to such an extent that we can already see ourselves in possession of the desired result."
And he supported it by declaring:
"The world wants your best, and you should resolve early in life never to give anything but the best of which you are capable."
What is your purpose here on earth? Few people know why they're here and what their destiny is, so

ATOMIC STEPS

they place very little value on their lives and the lives of others. It's amazing, though, to see the transformation that takes place as soon as a person discovers his true purpose in life — and takes up the challenge. Some people search all their lives and never find it, and others find it and refuse to accept it because they feel unworthy.

Moses, for one, felt inadequate when God called him to lead the children of Israel out of slavery. "But Moses said to God, 'I am not a great man! How can I go to the King and lead the Israelites out of Egypt?'" (Exod. 3:11) And yet, through eventual — although reluctant — willingness to accept God's call, with the aid of his brother, Aaron, Moses experienced a life filled with mountaintop experiences and miracles:

- His rod turned into a serpent in Pharaoh's presence (Exod. 7:10).

- Water turned into blood (Exod. 7:20).

- Frogs covered the land of Egypt (Exod. 8:5).

- The Lord struck down every Egyptian firstborn (Exod. 12:29).

- God parted the Red Sea (Exod. 14:21).

ATOMIC STEPS

- Manna fell from the sky (Exod. 16:15).

- Moses received the Ten Commandments, written with the finger of God, on Mt. Sinai (Exod. 31:18).

Moses' life changed from "Who am I?" to the recipient of the Ten Commandments from God's hand.

In Genesis 28:12, Jacob, who had stolen his brother's birthright, dreamed he saw a ladder set upon the earth, the top of it reaching heaven, with angels of God ascending and descending on it. "And behold the Lord stood above it, and said, 'I am the Lord God of Abraham thy father, and the God of Isaac: the land whereon thou liest, to thee will I give it, and to thy seed'." (Gen. 28:13 KJV) Jacob changed his life after he was forgivingly blessed by his father, Isaac (Gen. 28: 1) was rewarded with family and estate blessings. He also received a name change to "Israel" synonymous with blessings, after wrestling with God, (Gen. 32:22-32). Later when he came face to face with his brother Esau from whom he fled after forging the acceptance of his birthright, Jacob forgivingly sought to please Esau and even addressed him as *master*. Gen. 33:10-11 says: "Jacob said, 'No! Please! If I have pleased you, then accept the gift I give you. I'm happy to see your face again.

ATOMIC STEPS

It is like seeing the face of God because you have accepted me. So, I beg you to accept the gift I give you. God has been very good to me, and I have more than I need.' And because Jacob begged. Esau accepted the gift." What a change in the lives of both men!

At the top of this staircase, your transformation awaits you: A beautiful, enhanced life; others will seek you out to remold their lives and character. Will you trade your heart of stone for one of moldable clay and allow the Master Potter to work on you? If so, you're almost ready for the transformation you deserve. You will set the world on fire with your illumination. It will be all about what people see in you — not something you have to push on them or try to prove.

Changing your world — is your freedom ticket. You're about to discover the new you as you move forward with your life. But first, you must surrender your life to the Potter. And you also need to remove any emotional scars that alienate you from the life you're entitled to live.

If you have been hurt by someone in the past, you probably try to guard against future injury. In doing so, you form a "spiritual callus," which is like an emotional scar, to protect your ego. And that creates an emotional wall that no one can scale. A church member who has been the subject of wrongful

ATOMIC STEPS

criticism by a church leader may choose to never again attend that church or another house of worship.

In his book on *Psycho-Cybernetics*, Dr. Maxwell Maltz discusses removing the emotional scars in your life. To paraphrase Dr. Maltz:

- A child who has had his ego sliced up by a repressive and cruel parent or teacher vows to never trust another authority figure.

- A man whose love has been rejected by a woman vows to never again become romantically involved.

- A woman who has been hurt by one man vows to never trust another man again.

Dr. Maltz continues,

"As in the case of a facial scar, excessive protection against the source of injury can make us more vulnerable and do us more damage in other areas. The person who feels 'lonely' or out of touch with other human beings, also feels out of touch with his real self and with life."

The emotional wall you build as protection against one person can cut you off from other human beings and even from yourself.

ATOMIC STEPS

Emotional scars can create juvenile delinquents. Psychiatrist Bernard Holland said "that although juvenile delinquents appear to be independent and are known to brag — particularly about how they hate everyone in authority — they protest too much. Underneath this hard exterior, he says, "is a soft inner person who wants to depend on others."[4] However, they seem to not want to get close to anyone. They will not trust others and always seem to have their defense antennas up.

Emotional scars on our ego have another adverse effect. As Dr. Maltz explained, "They tend to lead to the development of a scarred, marred self-image; the picture of a person not liked or accepted by other human beings, the picture of a person who can't get along well in the world in which he lives."

Emotional scars prevent you from changing your life. They prevent you from becoming what professor of educational psychology Dr. Arthur W. Combs called a "self-fulfilled person." This should be your goal, he said, but it's not something with which you're born; it must be achieved. Jacob removed the emotional scar of stealing his brother's birthright by seeking forgiveness and was immensely blessed.

According to Dr. Maltz, self-fulfilled people have the following characteristics:

ATOMIC STEPS

- They see themselves as liked, wanted, acceptable, and able individuals.

- They have a high degree of acceptance for who they are.

- They have a feeling of oneness with others.

- They have a rich store of information and knowledge.

"The person with emotional scars not only has a self-image of an unwanted, unliked, and incapable person, but he also has an image of the world in which he lives as a hostile place,"
Maltz adds.
How do you change your self-image? By changing the way, you are.
Before I rededicated my life to the Lord almost five years ago, I struggled with my setbacks in life felt animosity toward everyone who had wronged me and wanted to see my family fall apart. However, it was not until I put everyone's name on a list and prayed individually for their forgiveness and mine that I received true freedom from my emotional imprisonment. Today, my life is one of fullness and

ATOMIC STEPS

trust because I've allowed change to permeate my entire being.

A car's rearview mirror is smaller than its windshield for a reason. Yet most people spend their lives looking through their rearview mirror. Unconditional forgiveness will release you from the vice of your enemies and set you up for success. Your changed life is beckoning.

God wants to bless you. He's standing at the door to usher you in.

"Come unto me, all ye that labor and are heavy laden, and I will give you rest."
(Matt. 11:28)

By surrendering your will to Him, you are automatically placing Him in the driver's seat of your life. And He knows every pothole, intersection, and traffic signal.

The world has been searching for you. It needs people who will step up and stand in the gap — those who aren't afraid to step off the sidelines and into the game. You've acquired knowledge and wisdom among these pages, and the past can no longer hold you in its cocoon. By changing who you are, you've equipped yourself to change your world. These steps help you breathe victory daily. You may not be Winston Churchill, Martin Luther King Jr., Abraham Lincoln, Helen Keller, Rosa Parks, Mother Teresa, Columbus, Moses, or Jacob. But you are YOU

ATOMIC STEPS

— right here, right now. Will you of strong character embrace the world? What could *you* do with the determination of some of the personalities? Will this world become a better place because *you* embrace change?

I hope that, by now, you've found a cause greater than yourself and are ready to take charge of your destiny. Dr. King said:

"If a man hasn't discovered something that he will die for, he isn't fit to live."

YOU are chosen, and the world needs you.

21

LEGACY DEFINED

For what do I want to be remembered? This is a fundamental question asked by just about every successful individual. Like the caterpillar going through the cocoon to become a beautiful butterfly, equally, all truly victorious people go through walls, which stand in their way towards their destiny. They will also tell you that their success principles were rooted, deep down, inside of them and were the defining elements that helped create the success that you see all around them. If you nurture those roots that run deep within you, your chance of succeeding is inevitable.

ATOMIC STEPS

In 2009 Senator Barack Obama was elected as America's first black president. Obama, who rose to great success, grew up during the civil rights revolution of the 1960s when blacks were not permitted to ride in the front of the bus as whites did, dine in certain restaurants, or even be permitted to vote. In that era "segregation" was not only an academic institutional slogan but rather an uncomfortable household word to the Negro race. The fundamental reason, back then severe limits were placed on the associations of these two races - with blacks at a stringent disadvantage. Obama went through those walls and consequently, earned the American vote.

During that civil rights era of intense racial conflicts, leaders such as Malcolm X and Dr. Martin Luther King Jr. emerged on the scene. King, a black man from the South fought for, and lost his life (assassinated) daring to fulfill his dream of equality. A dream that: One day his children would not be judged by the color of their skin but by the content of their character. In addition: one day all children regardless of the color of their skin will live together in unity.

Kamala Harris, a female Senator from California has been elected the first woman Vice President of the US. Our change is constantly extending its hand.

ATOMIC STEPS

Oprah Winfrey was born in Mississippi at a time when segregation in that state denied basic civil rights to African Americans. She came from a home with no electricity and drinking water, also a victim of a troubled youth. As a child she was required to read books and every two weeks, to draft a report about what she had read. Oprah would often say that she wanted to make her living by talking. She was a gifted, quick-witted speaker.

In 1972 she became the first Black woman to hold the anchor position at Nashville's WTVF-TV. In 1986 she launched the Oprah Winfrey Show. In 1994 she bought her studio "Harpo." In 1996 she began Oprah's Book Club to promote reading, for which she recommends a recently published book each month. She sets aside one show each month for a full discussion on the book. She has since created her classic book club, which features three authors per annum. Oprah regularly gives 10% of her income to charities, mostly having to do with youth, education, and books.

Oprah Winfrey, who became a billionaire at age 49, has not only risen to become the most powerful and influential woman in the television world but also ruler of a large entertainment and communications empire - from a life of poverty and abuse to a life of greatness. Oprah Winfrey at one point in her broadcast career believed in herself so much that

ATOMIC STEPS

sources close to her knew that she was like a hit record to be released. It wasn't long before she became that hit record. She has broken down so many walls. Now when she talks - people listen.

Is your destiny a cause greater than yourself? Is it a life of boundlessness?

There are things you and I will accomplish in our lifetime that will not only affect our relatives, friends, neighbors, and co-workers but also our enemies alike. It has been discovered that 90% of an iceberg rests beneath the surface. It may surprise you that each of us has at least 90% of our potential lying untapped. As human beings, we are known to use only that other 10% of our potential.

In my interaction with successful people from all levels of society, I have discovered that they are not only specialists in their field but that they had at one point in their lives said yes to their potential. In my journey up the ladder of success, I've learned to become "a sponge" by learning from them; I've worn their shoes and felt some of their pain. You will meet most of them as well as me through these pages. Most of all because success leaves clues, you will discover that as human beings, they recognized their value, believed in their value, and increased their value. Consequently, they've become valuable. Our world has been searching for you. It needs people who are willing to step off the sidelines and

ATOMIC STEPS

into the game. It needs individuals to make a significant difference.

ATOMIC STEPS

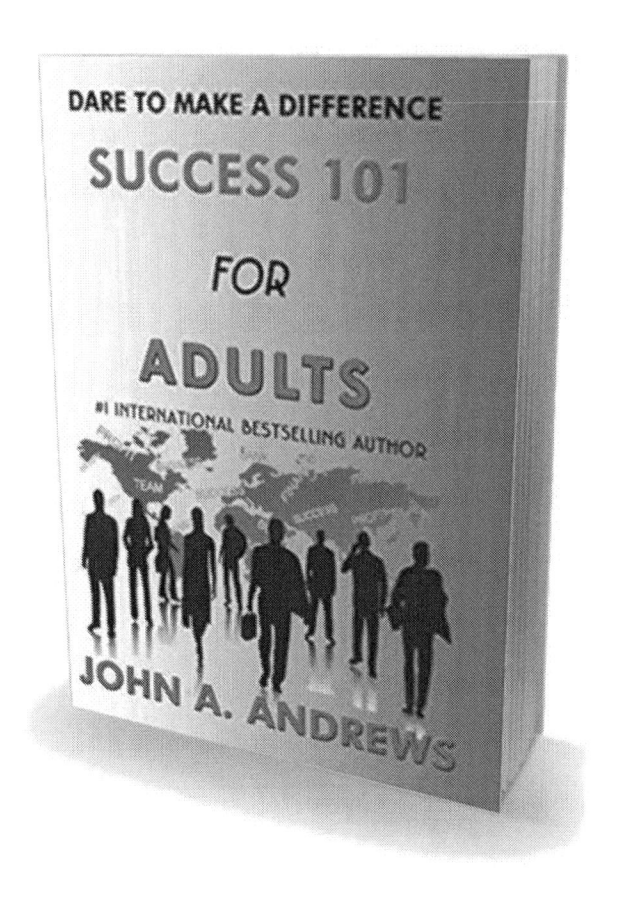

DARE TO MAKE A DIFFERENCE

SUCCESS 101

FOR

ADULTS

#1 INTERNATIONAL BESTSELLING AUTHOR

JOHN A. ANDREWS

ATOMIC STEPS

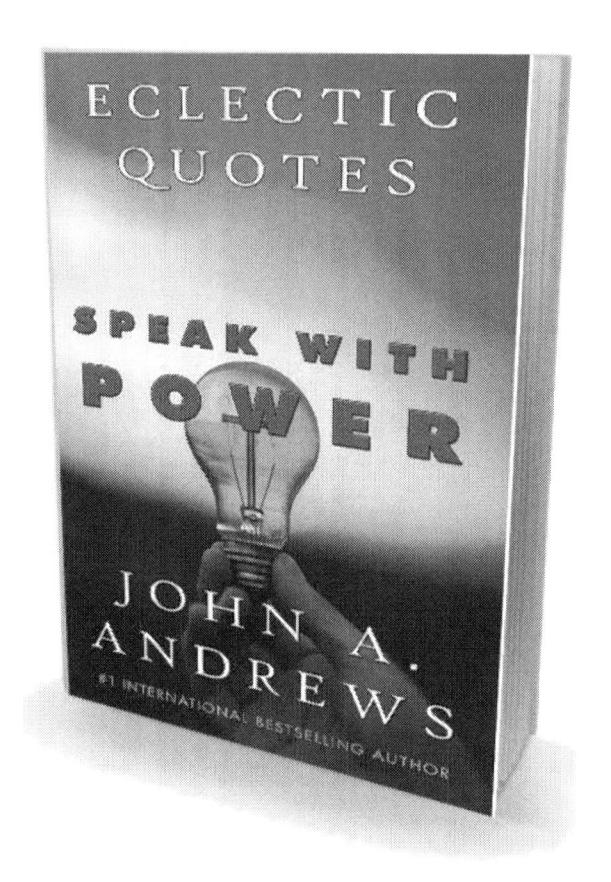

ATOMIC STEPS

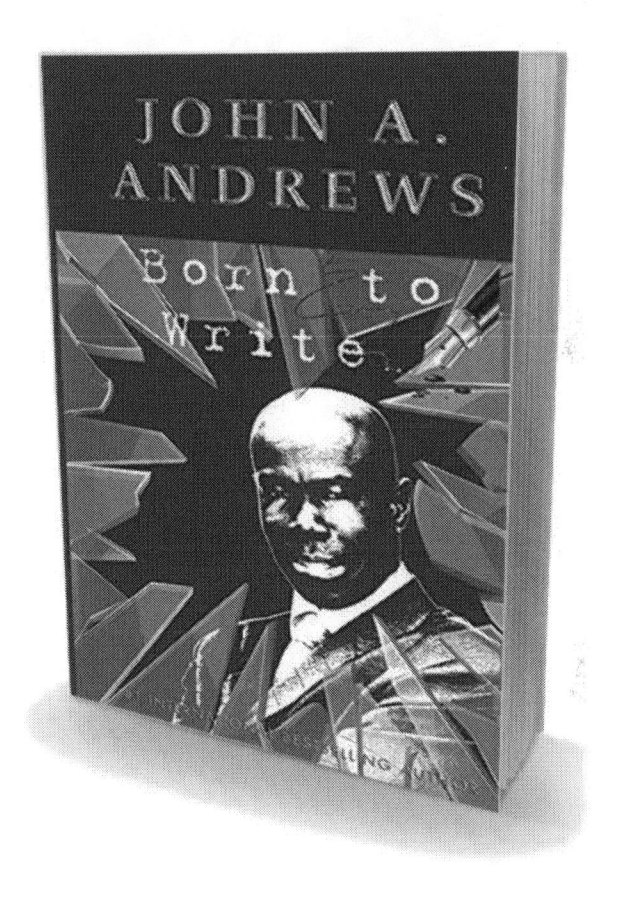

ATOMIC STEPS

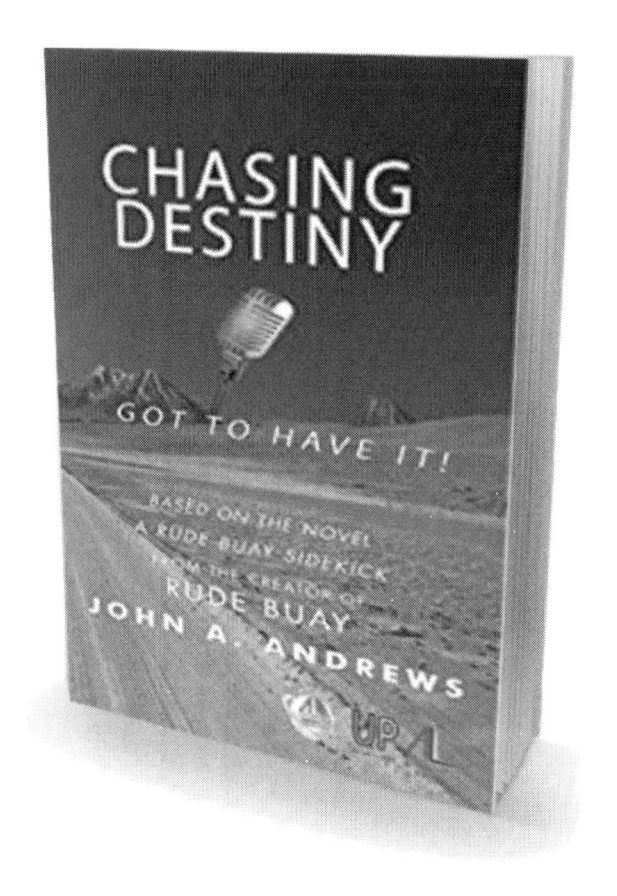

ATOMIC STEPS

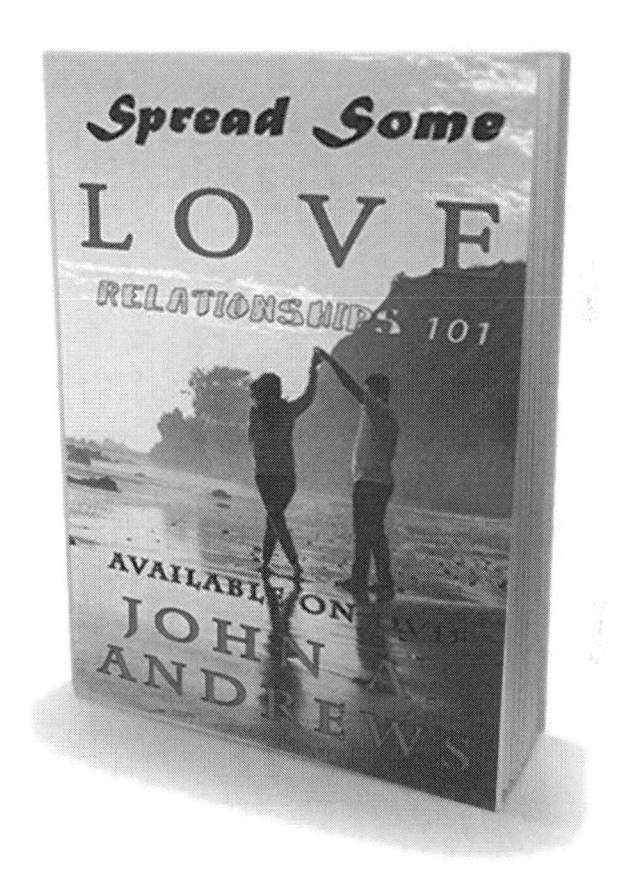

ATOMIC STEPS

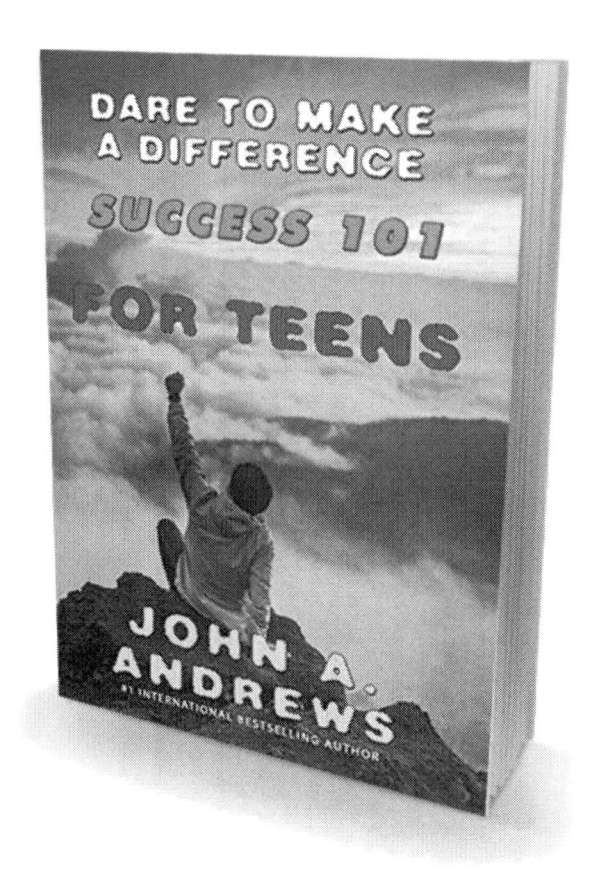

ATOMIC STEPS

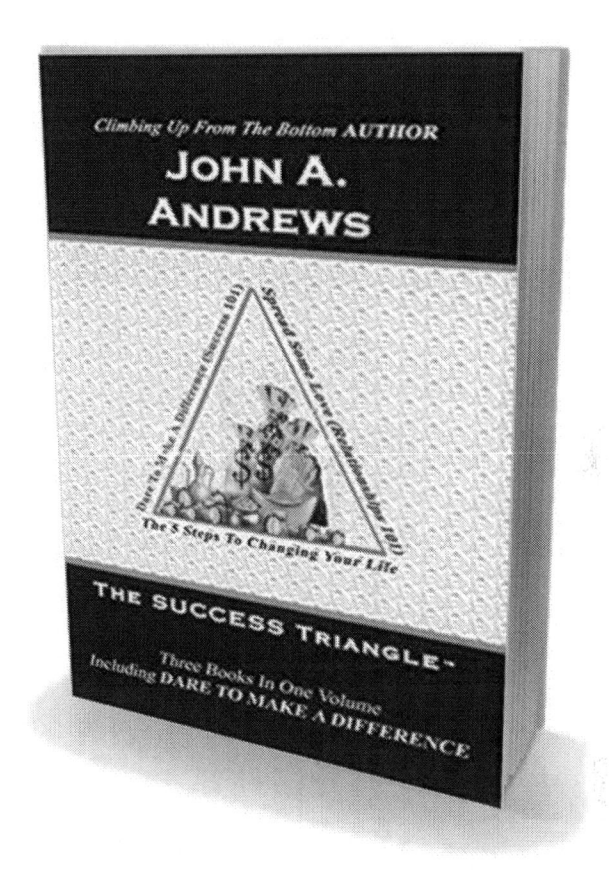

ATOMIC STEPS

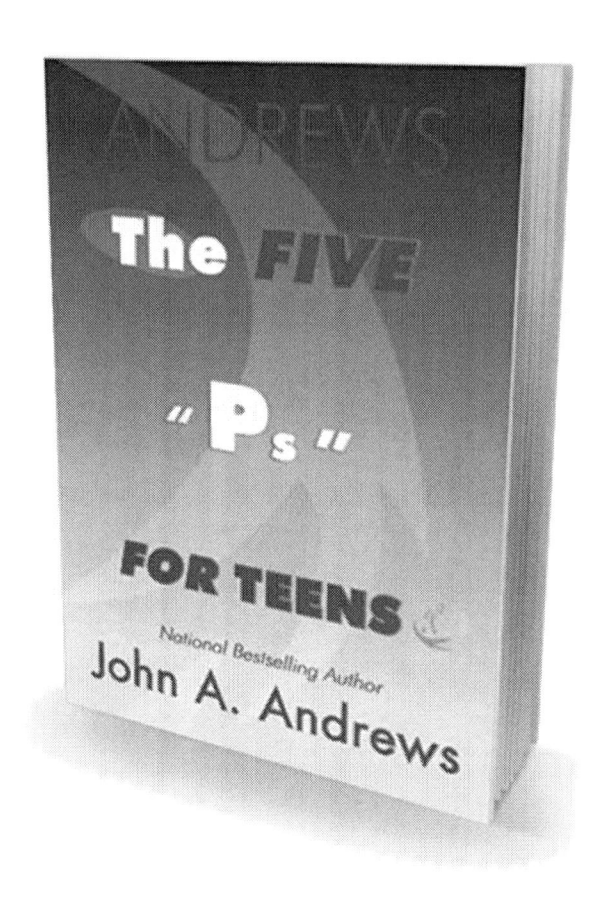

ATOMIC STEPS

ATOMIC STEPS

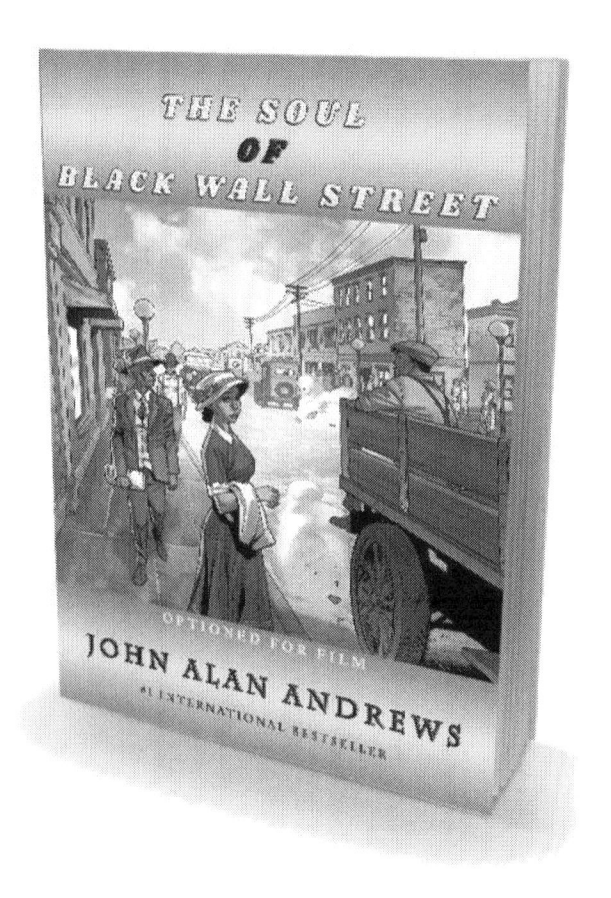

ATOMIC STEPS

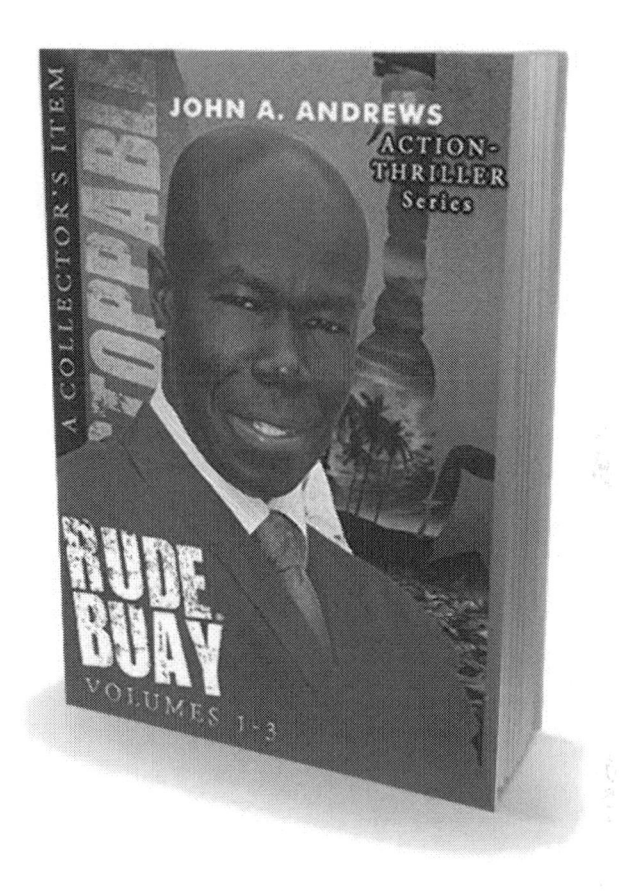

ATOMIC STEPS

THE PIPS®

ALIPNET® ORIGINAL

Made in the USA
Middletown, DE
19 November 2023